RAND ARROYO CENTER

The U.S. Military Response to the 2010 Haiti Earthquake

Considerations for Army Leaders

Gary Cecchine, Forrest E. Morgan, Michael A. Wermuth,
Timothy Jackson, Agnes Gereben Schaefer, Matthew Stafford

Prepared for the United States Army
Approved for public release; distribution unlimited

The research described in this report was sponsored by the United States Army under Contract No. W74V8H-06-C-0001.

Library of Congress Cataloging-in-Publication Data is available for this publication.

ISBN: 978-0-8330-8075-2

RAND OFFICES

SANTA MONICA, CA • WASHINGTON, DC

PITTSBURGH, PA • NEW ORLEANS, LA • JACKSON, MS • BOSTON, MA

DOHA, QA • CAMBRIDGE, UK • BRUSSELS, BE

www.rand.org

Preface

This report describes how the U.S. military responded to the 2010 earthquake that devastated Haiti, and it presents recommendations for improving military foreign humanitarian assistance and disaster relief. The report should be of interest throughout the Department of Defense, as well as to other organizations involved in such assistance and relief operations.

The report summarizes the results of a research project called "Improving the Army's Disaster Response: Lessons from the Earthquake in Haiti," sponsored by the Deputy Chief of Staff, G-8, Headquarters, Department of the Army. The purpose of the project was to prepare an account of military operations in response to the earthquake, considering planning, doctrine, and execution, in order to identify challenges faced and make recommendations to improve the conduct of similar missions in the future. Related RAND research has been published in the following reports:

- Lynn E. Davis, Jill Rough, Gary Cecchine, Agnes Gereben Schaefer, and Laurinda L. Rohn, *Hurricane Katrina: Lessons for Army Planning and Operations*, MG-603-A, 2007
- Lynn E. Davis, David E. Mosher, Rick Brennan Jr., Michael D. Greenberg, K. Scott McMahon, and Charles W. Yost, *Army Forces for Homeland Security*, MG-221-A, 2004
- Gary Cecchine, Michael A. Wermuth, Roger C. Molander, K. Scott McMahon, Jesse D. Malkin, Jennifer Brower, John D. Woodward, and Donna F. Barbisch, *Triage for Civil Support:*

Using Military Medical Assets to Respond to Terrorist Attacks, Santa Monica, Calif.: RAND Corporation, MG-217-OSD, 2004.

This research was sponsored by the Deputy Chief of Staff, G-8, Headquarters, Department of the Army, and conducted within the RAND Arroyo Center's Strategy, Doctrine, and Resources Program. RAND Arroyo Center, part of the RAND Corporation, is a federally funded research and development center sponsored by the United States Army.

The Project Unique Identification Code (PUIC) for the project that produced this document is HQDA105620.

For more information on RAND Arroyo Center, contact the Director of Operations (telephone 310-393-0411, extension 6419; fax 310-451-6952; email Marcy_Agmon@rand.org) or visit Arroyo's website at http://www.rand.org/ard/.

Contents

Figures and Table

Figures

Table

Summary

The 7.0-magnitude earthquake that struck Haiti on January 12, 2010, collapsed 100,000 structures, damaged 200,000 more, killed more than 316,000 people, injured 300,000 others, and displaced more than 1 million people. It virtually decapitated the Haitian government, destroying the presidential palace and 14 of 16 government ministries and claiming the lives of numerous government officials and employees, as well as the head of mission of the United Nations Stabilization Mission in Haiti (MINUSTAH) and his principal deputy.

Shortly after the earthquake, surviving officials of the government of Haiti (GoH) made an urgent request for U.S. assistance. In reply, President Barack Obama promised U.S. support, directing a "whole-of-government" response led by the U.S. Agency for International Development (USAID) with significant support from the U.S. Department of Defense (DoD) through U.S. Southern Command (SOUTHCOM). Selected U.S. military elements began mobilizing immediately, and, on January 14, SOUTHCOM established Joint Task Force (JTF)–Haiti (JTF-Haiti) to provide U.S. military support to the international response and relief effort through Operation Unified Response. U.S. Army forces constituted a principal component of JTF-Haiti. Operation Unified Response rendered the stricken nation humanitarian assistance (HA) and disaster relief (DR) until June 1, 2010, when JTF-Haiti stood down and all remaining U.S. forces were withdrawn except for a small coordination cell.

This report examines how JTF-Haiti supported the HA/DR effort in Haiti. It focuses on how JTF-Haiti was organized, how it conducted Operation Unified Response, and how the Army supported that effort. The analysis includes a review of existing authorities and organizations and explains how JTF-Haiti fit into the U.S. "whole-of-government" approach, as well as the international response. The purpose of the study was to assess the effectiveness of JTF-Haiti, with the goal of informing the U.S. Army on how to best prepare for and support future HA/DR operations.

The study revealed that JTF-Haiti provided prompt assistance to many thousands of earthquake victims in a DR operation of enormous size and complexity. The operation was unquestionably effective in that many more lives would doubtless have been lost without the assistance of JTF-Haiti. The speed that made Operation Unified Response successful may have been obtained at some cost in efficiency and acceptance of risk, but those costs and risks were mitigated by the decisive leadership provided by the JTF-Haiti commander, LTG P. K. (Ken) Keen, and a serendipitous set of circumstances favoring the relief effort. Those circumstances included General Keen's presence in Haiti when the disaster occurred; his long-standing, positive professional relationship with the MINUSTAH military commander; the survival of the U.S. ambassador's residence and U.S. Embassy in Haiti, with their communication equipment intact; and the availability of key U.S. Army capabilities for immediate deployment to Haiti.

How the United States Responded at the National Level

The levels of damage and human suffering from the Haiti earthquake seriously complicated U.S. efforts to render HA/DR. President Obama immediately pledged U.S. support and designated USAID as lead federal agency for coordinating the U.S. response. The USAID Office of U.S. Foreign Disaster Assistance (OFDA) stood up a Response Management Team on January 12, the day of the earthquake, and deployed a Disaster Assistance Response Team (DART) to Haiti the following day. On January 14, the Chairman of the Joint Chiefs of Staff issued an execute order authorizing U.S. military forces to commence operations, and SOUTHCOM stood up JTF-Haiti and appointed SOUTHCOM Military Deputy Commander, General Keen, as its commander.

Given the magnitude of the disaster and the whole-of-government approach directed by the President, the White House and National Security Council took an active role in providing policy direction, and an interagency task force was assembled in Washington to coordinate interdepartmental efforts. The State Department was significantly involved in executing policy direction from the White House and ensuring that appropriate funding was available to U.S. entities. Meanwhile, USAID stood up an Office of the Response Coordinator in Haiti to help coordinate interagency efforts on the ground. And although State and Defense were the most-prominent departments supporting relief operations, numerous other departments and agencies were also heavily involved in the effort.

The U.S. Military Response to the Haiti Earthquake

The response to the 2010 Haiti earthquake was the U.S. military's largest international DR effort in history, and the U.S. military was the single largest contributor to the overall effort in terms of personnel and capabilities. The response was tailored to the conditions present on the ground in Haiti at the time of the disaster. Because MINUSTAH was already conducting substantial security and stability operations there, U.S. leaders, in consultation with United Nations (UN) officials and the GoH, decided that SOUTHCOM would create JTF-Haiti as a separate U.S. entity instead of establishing an additional *combined* JTF (CJTF; sometimes also called a coalition JTF) that might lead to confusion over roles and authorities or undermine MINUSTAH's credibility. JTF-Haiti would carry out Operation Unified Response in coordination with MINUSTAH.

Establishing Joint Task Force–Haiti

Within hours of the earthquake, DoD sent a warning order to SOUTHCOM and supporting organizations to prepare for HA/DR operations. This prompted a series of immediate actions in

SOUTHCOM and other military headquarters. General Keen was visiting the residence of U.S. Ambassador to Haiti Kenneth H. Merten at the time of the quake, and he and Ambassador Merten began relaying communications between the GoH, the U.S. government, and SOUTHCOM from the onset of the disaster. After receiving the GoH request for assistance, General Keen immediately began requesting the deployment of U.S. military forces and coordinating U.S. military efforts with other countries and relief organizations. Given his presence and direct involvement, General Keen was appointed commander of JTF-Haiti when it was stood up two days later. In his discussions with the GoH, SOUTHCOM, and UN representatives in Haiti, it was agreed that MINUSTAH would continue to provide security and stability and that JTF-Haiti would focus on providing HA/DR. These efforts faced immediate challenges. The major airports and seaports had been destroyed, and streets in the nation's capital, Port-au-Prince, were choked with rubble.

Because of the magnitude of the disaster and the urgency of response, General Keen chose not to wait for the formal process for determining requirements and tailoring forces for HA/DR, and no formal assessment was done at the beginning of Operation Unified Response. Instead, General Keen relied on his judgment as a senior U.S. military commander and implemented verbal orders of commanding officer (VOCOs) to assemble the capabilities and resources he believed he would need to begin operations. The first units assigned to JTF-Haiti included several U.S. naval vessels and the Global Response Force (GRF).[1] Before those units began arriving on January 14, the Air Force Special Operations Command 1st Special Operations Wing reopened Haiti's international airport. U.S. Coast Guard (USCG) vessels also arrived on the scene early and began delivering emergency supplies and evacuating U.S. citizens. The flow of forces increased between

[1] The GRF is a designated U.S. Army unit put on round-the-clock alert for immediate deployment to conduct combat operations anywhere in the world within 96 hours. At the time of the Haiti earthquake, the GRF was 2 Brigade Combat Team, 82nd Airborne Division.

January 16 and January 21 as such units as the 22nd Marine Expeditionary Unit and more U.S. Navy ships began to arrive.

Phasing in Operation Unified Response

The original execute order for the conduct of Operation Unified Response envisioned five distinct phases for the U.S. military HA/DR operations in Haiti:

- phase I (initial response)
- phase II (relief operations)
- phase III (restoration)
- phase IV (stabilization)
- phase V (recovery).

In phase I, the initial response, JTF-Haiti focused on saving lives, providing relief to survivors, and coordinating response activities with MINUSTAH and numerous nongovernmental organizations (NGOs). At the peak of the military response, on January 31, 2010, JTF-Haiti included more than 22,200 personnel, 33 U.S. Navy and USCG vessels, and more than 300 aircraft. During the first three weeks of Operation Unified Response, the VOCO process facilitated a rapid "push" of people and capabilities into JTF-Haiti but also resulted in responders arriving without full situational awareness and direction. Moreover, the lack of any formal requirements assessment may have resulted in additional inefficiencies.

On February 5, JTF-Haiti transitioned from initial response operations to phase II, relief operations, with priorities shifting to assistance for internally displaced persons (IDPs) through World Food Programme sites and continuing collaboration with the GoH, NGOs, and MINUSTAH.

In the middle of March, Operation Unified Response entered phase III, a period of support to the restoration of the GoH. During this period, the JTF headquarters staff was replaced, and General Keen turned command over to his deputy commander, Major General Simeon G. Trombitas. Activities in which JTF personnel were involved expanded somewhat to include preparations for potential floods and mudslides. However, JTF-Haiti turned over responsibility for many of the support functions it had been performing to partners in the GoH and MINUSTAH.

The stabilization operation planned as phase IV of Operation Unified Response was not carried out. Throughout the relief effort, the citizens of Haiti conducted themselves with admirable order and civility, and MINUSTAH security forces proved capable of handling the minor breaches of the peace that did occur. Therefore, SOUTHCOM and JTF-Haiti, in coordination with MINUSTAH and GoH officials, determined that U.S. forces would not need to execute Operation Unified Response phase IV.

In late May, JTF-Haiti proceeded to phase V, recovery, in preparation for a full transition of duties to the GoH. Over the course of the operation, U.S. forces had been steadily withdrawn from phase II onward, and only a small contingent of U.S. military police and engineers remained when Operation Unified Response terminated on June 1, 2010.

Joint Task Force–Haiti's Coordination with Other Major Actors

The massive relief effort required JTF-Haiti to coordinate with many government agencies and NGOs, U.S. and foreign. Twenty-six countries provided significant military assets in support of the earthquake response, including field hospitals, troops, military aircraft, hospital ships, cargo ships, port handling equipment, and helicopters. Given the U.S. decision not to establish a CJTF, JTF-Haiti created a humanitarian assistance coordination center through which it could coordinate its efforts with interagency, intergovernmental, multinational, and NGO partners. Similarly, MINUSTAH established a joint operations and tasking center (JOTC) to serve as a single point of contact for requests for military or police assistance. The long-standing relationship between the MINUSTAH commander and the JTF-Haiti commander greatly facilitated coordination between the two organizations. SOUTHCOM and JTF-Haiti used unclassified information and public platforms whenever possible to facilitate the exchange of information across partners.

By all accounts, JTF-Haiti developed good working relationships with USAID and the OFDA DART, as well as with other interagency partners. The U.S. military played a vital role in supporting almost 1,000 NGOs in their relief efforts in Haiti, which included IDP camps, food and shelter distributions, and medical facilities. JTF-Haiti integrated well in the systems and processes of the NGOs, especially by providing liaison officers to the JOTC and participating in the UN "clusters."[2] In this regard, JTF-Haiti provided much-needed support to the lead federal agency, USAID, which lacked sufficient staffing to fully integrate its representatives into the many UN and NGO relief activities under way in Haiti.

General Observations

Four broad themes stand out in JTF-Haiti's experience in coordinating with U.S. interagency partners, international organizations, foreign militaries, and the NGO community. First, the Haiti experience reinforces the general notion that, during DR, communication can be facilitated if the different players have relationships already in place. Second, JTF-Haiti's success in sharing information with other countries and NGOs was largely due to the fact that it did not classify most of that information. Third, because of their experience in civil affairs in recent operations in Iraq and Afghanistan, the U.S. Army members of JTF-Haiti appeared to have been well prepared for interacting with

---

[2] The cluster system is a means by which like functional-area experts from participating relief organizations regularly gather to coordinated problem solving. It was introduced as part of the UN Emergency Relief Coordinator's 2005 reform of the UN humanitarian relief system. This approach tries to clarify the division of labor among organizations and better define roles and responsibilities within the key sectors of the response. Response efforts are currently organized around 11 clusters: logistics; nutrition; emergency shelter; camp management and coordination; health; protection; agriculture; emergency telecommunications; early recovery; education; and water, sanitation, and hygiene. UN and NGO specialists in each of these areas meet periodically (typically daily) in clusters to coordinate efforts and exchange support and ideas.

earthquake victims in Haiti. Fourth, the strengths and weaknesses of the UN JOTC should be examined in depth to determine whether this is a model that should be used in future DRs.

Findings and Recommendations

The United States made major contributions to the multinational relief effort in Haiti, and the U.S. Army played a key role in that response, saving lives and easing suffering. But improvements could be made that would reduce the challenges so that future relief efforts might be conducted more efficiently and effectively. These findings and recommendations are offered to the multiple levels of DoD policymaking and direction responsible for HA/DR operations.

Findings

1. Ample U.S. legal authority exists for the military to engage in foreign HA/DR operations, but the key DoD policy needs to be updated. The version of the DoD directive (DoDD) for such activities, DoDD 5100.46, that was in effect at the time of the Haiti earthquake was significantly out of date.[3] Although that did not hinder the accomplishment of Operation Unified Response, updating the DoDD will ensure that similar missions in the future have the appropriate, current supporting policies and direction.
2. Mass and initiative enabled a prompt, robust response. The JTF-Haiti commander's informal approach to determining initial requirements and his aggressive use of VOCO for force selection and assignment resulted in a high volume of people and resources being assigned to the relief effort quickly, and U.S. military leaders were given significant latitude to exercise initiative in directing the response effort.

---

[3] This discussion refers to the 1975 DoDD, which was in force during the response to the Haiti earthquake, and it has since been revised.

3. Planning and coordination shortfalls hindered efficiency. The relief effort in Haiti was accomplished without the benefit of well-established plans within SOUTHCOM for such a mission, and the SOUTHCOM staff was not initially organized to optimize the support that a large-scale military effort, such as Operation Unified Response, required. Moreover, the informal, top-down process that pushed resources to the effort so quickly generated inefficiencies that might have impaired the operation's effectiveness. However, whether such inefficiencies had a substantial effect on mission accomplishment could not be determined because the lack of formal, condition-based planning at the outset of Operation Unified Response made it impossible to establish metrics with which to measure JTF-Haiti's performance.
4. JTF-Haiti owed much of its success to serendipity. Numerous factors contributed to Operation Unified Response's success. Operation Unified Response was defined by a singular set of circumstances that may have worked to the advantage of JTF-Haiti, including the fact that the SOUTHCOM deputy commander was in Haiti and at the U.S. ambassador's residence when the earthquake struck; the ambassador's residence withstood the earthquake, and the communication equipment there remained functional; General Keen was a longtime colleague of the MINUSTAH commander, facilitating early and continual coordination; the GRF was available for rapid deployment to JTF-Haiti; the JTF-Haiti commander had a positive professional relationship with the 18th Airborne Corps commander, enabling him to arrange for the immediate deployment of a much-needed headquarters element to lead the JTF; and many soldiers and marines assigned to JTF-Haiti had a high level of experience in civil affairs and other aspects of working with local citizens.

Recommendations

1. Update the DoDD for foreign HA/DR to better describe the statutory and organizational changes that have taken place since

its last publication and provide important policy guidance to DoD entities and their partners.

2. Create a national framework for foreign HA/DR similar to the National Response Framework in place for domestic incidents. A national framework for U.S. foreign HA/DR could document and guide a whole-of-government approach for U.S. efforts and facilitate related planning, training, and exercises.
3. Ensure that all senior Army commanders are familiar with the guidance provided in the recently published *Department of Defense Support to Foreign Disaster Relief (Handbook for JTF Commanders and Below)* (Office of the Deputy Assistant Secretary of Defense for Partnership Strategy and Stability Operations, 2011). This handbook should be required reading at U.S. Army intermediate and senior service schools.
4. Consider a standing organization to help develop HA/DR doctrine; facilitate HA/DR planning, training, and exercises; establish HA/DR metrics; monitor preparedness and availability of specialized HA/DR units and personnel; provide a base for HA/DR expertise; assist with interagency, intergovernmental, and nongovernmental collaboration; conduct initial assessments of HA/DR requirements; and maintain historical data on HA/DR operations. Models that could be considered for a standing organization include the following:
    a. joint interagency task force
    b. DoD Standing JTF for HA/DR
    c. Canadian Forces Disaster Assistance Response Team.

Acknowledgments

We thank Timothy Muchmore, director of the Army Quadrennial Defense Review Office (G-8), for sponsoring this project and for his guidance. COL Sylvester Brown, then also of the Army Quadrennial Defense Review Office, was instrumental in supporting the research effort and providing expert advice. We thank our RAND colleagues Laurinda L. Rohn for her leadership and advice and Edward W. Chan, Jefferson P. Marquis, and Karl P. Mueller for their expert review and advice on the manuscript. Dallas Owens also provided a very helpful review. Melissa Ko and Maria Falvo provided outstanding support in compiling this document.

Any errors or oversights are ours alone.

Abbreviations

ACP	assault command post
AD	airborne division
AFSOC	Air Force Special Operations Command
AMCIT	U.S. citizen
AOR	area of responsibility
APAN	All Partners Access Network
ARSOUTH	U.S. Army South
BATARG	USS *Bataan* Amphibious Ready Group
BCT	brigade combat team
CA	civil affairs
CBP	U.S. Customs and Border Protection
CBRNE	chemical, biological, radiological, nuclear, or high-yield explosive
CDC	Centers for Disease Control and Prevention
CJCS	Chairman of the Joint Chiefs of Staff
CJTF	combined joint task force
COCOM	combatant command

DART	disaster assistance response team
DCHA	Bureau for Democracy, Conflict, and Humanitarian Assistance
DCO/DIR	deputy commander, operations; director
DHS	U.S. Department of Homeland Security
DMAT	disaster medical assistance team
DMORT	disaster mortuary operational response team
DoD	U.S. Department of Defense
DoDD	Department of Defense directive
DoDI	Department of Defense instruction
DR	disaster relief
DSCA	Defense Security Cooperation Agency
ESF	Emergency Support Function
EXORD	execute order
FEMA	Federal Emergency Management Agency
FY	fiscal year
GAO	U.S. Government Accountability Office
GCC	geographic combatant commander
GoH	government of Haiti
GRF	Global Response Force
HA	humanitarian assistance
HACC	humanitarian assistance coordination center
HAST	humanitarian assistance survey team

HHS	U.S. Department of Health and Human Services
ICE	U.S. Immigration and Customs Enforcement
IDP	internally displaced person
IMSURT	International Medical Surgical Response Team
ISR	intelligence, surveillance, and reconnaissance
JFHQ	joint force headquarters
JIATF	joint interagency task force
JOTC	joint operations and tasking center
JP	joint publication
JTF	joint task force
JTF-Haiti	Joint Task Force–Haiti
JTF-PO	Joint Task Force–Port Opening
LNO	liaison officer
MINUSTAH	United Nations Stabilization Mission in Haiti
MITAM	mission tasking matrix
NASA	National Aeronautics and Space Administration
NDMS	National Disaster Medical System
NGO	nongovernmental organization
n-hour	time of notification
NRCC	National Response Coordination Center

NRF	National Response Framework
NSC	National Security Council
OCHA	Office for the Coordination of Humanitarian Affairs
OFDA	Office of U.S. Foreign Disaster Assistance
OHDACA	Overseas Humanitarian Disaster and Civic Aid
ORC	Office of the Response Coordinator
ORSA	operations research and systems analysis
OSD	Office of the Secretary of Defense
PCC	Policy Coordinating Committee
RFA	request for assistance
RMT	response management team
RSO	regional security officer
SecDef	Secretary of Defense
SECSTATE	Secretary of State
SJFHQ	Standing Joint Force Headquarters
SOUTHCOM	U.S. Southern Command
SOW	special operations wing
STS	special tactics squadron
TSA	Transportation Security Administration
UN	United Nations
UN-CMCoord	United Nations Civil-Military Coordination
USAID	U.S. Agency for International Development

USAR	urban search and rescue
USCG	U.S. Coast Guard
USCGC	U.S. Coast Guard cutter
USCIS	U.S. Citizenship and Immigration Services
USGS	U.S. Geological Survey
USJFCOM	U.S. Joint Forces Command
USNORTHCOM	U.S. Northern Command
USNS	U.S. Navy ship
USPACOM	U.S. Pacific Command
USSOCOM	U.S. Special Operations Command
VJ2	Vice Director for Intelligence, Joint Staff
VOCO	verbal orders of commanding officer
VTC	video teleconference
WARNORD	warning order
x-hour	time of warning order

CHAPTER ONE

Introduction

Background

The earthquake that struck Haiti in 2010 was one of the most devastating natural disasters in recent history, and it occurred in an impoverished country that already faced significant challenges of governance. As Table 1.1 indicates and Figure 1.1 illustrates, the 7.0-magnitude earthquake that struck in the afternoon of January 12 caused the greatest loss of life on record due to an earthquake in the Western Hemisphere and at least the fourth-greatest death toll of any natural disaster in the world in the past 100 years.[1] It collapsed 100,000 structures and damaged 200,000 more, killing more than 316,000 people, injuring 300,000 others, and displacing more than 1 million people (USAID, 2010d; U.S. Geological Survey [USGS], 2012). The response to the quake was hampered by the unfortunate decapitation of the Haitian government: The presidential palace and 14 of 16 government ministries were destroyed, claiming the lives of numerous government officials and employees. The head of mission of the United Nations (UN) Stabilization Mission in Haiti (MINUSTAH) and his principal deputy were killed when the mission's headquarters collapsed.[2]

[1] The Haiti earthquake's mortality ranking could be as high as the second worst, depending on what figures are accepted for the first two disasters listed in the table. Figures posted on the low side were provided by the government of China and are disputed by some independent authorities.

[2] Eighteen nations, including the United States, make up the military component of the UN mission in Haiti.

Table 1.1
The World's 15 Deadliest Natural Disasters Since 1900

Disaster	Death Toll[a]	Year	Country
Yangtze–Yellow River floods	50,000–4,000,000	1931	China
Tangshan earthquake	242,419–779,000	1976	China
Bhola cyclone	500,000	1970	East Pakistan
Haiti earthquake	316,000	2010	Haiti
Indian Ocean earthquake and tsunami	225,000–275,000	2004	Indonesia
Haiyuan earthquake	200,000–273,400	1920	China
Xining earthquake	200,000	1927	China
Great Kanto earthquake	143,000	1923	Japan
Yangtze River flood	140,000	1935	China
Cyclone Nargis	100,000–138,000	2008	Burma
Bangladesh cyclone	138,000	1991	Bangladesh
Messina earthquake and tsunami	123,000	1908	Italy
Ashgabat earthquake	110,000	1948	Turkmenistan
Floods around Hanoi	100,000	1971	North Vietnam
Yangtze flood	100,000	1911	China

SOURCES: "The World's Worst Natural Disasters," 2010; USGS, 2012.

NOTE: This list does not include droughts or famines, some of which have lasted for years and have caused higher death tolls over time.

[a] These figures are approximations. Where ranges are listed, significantly different totals have been reported by different sources.

Shortly after the earthquake, surviving officials of the government of Haiti (GoH) made an urgent request for U.S. assistance. In reply, President Barack Obama promised U.S. support, directing a "whole-of-government" response led by the U.S. Agency for International Development (USAID), with significant support from the U.S. Department of Defense (DoD). The DoD mission was given to U.S. Southern Command (SOUTHCOM), the U.S. combatant command (COCOM) responsible for Haiti's geographic region.

Figure 1.1
The World's 15 Deadliest Natural Disasters Since 1900

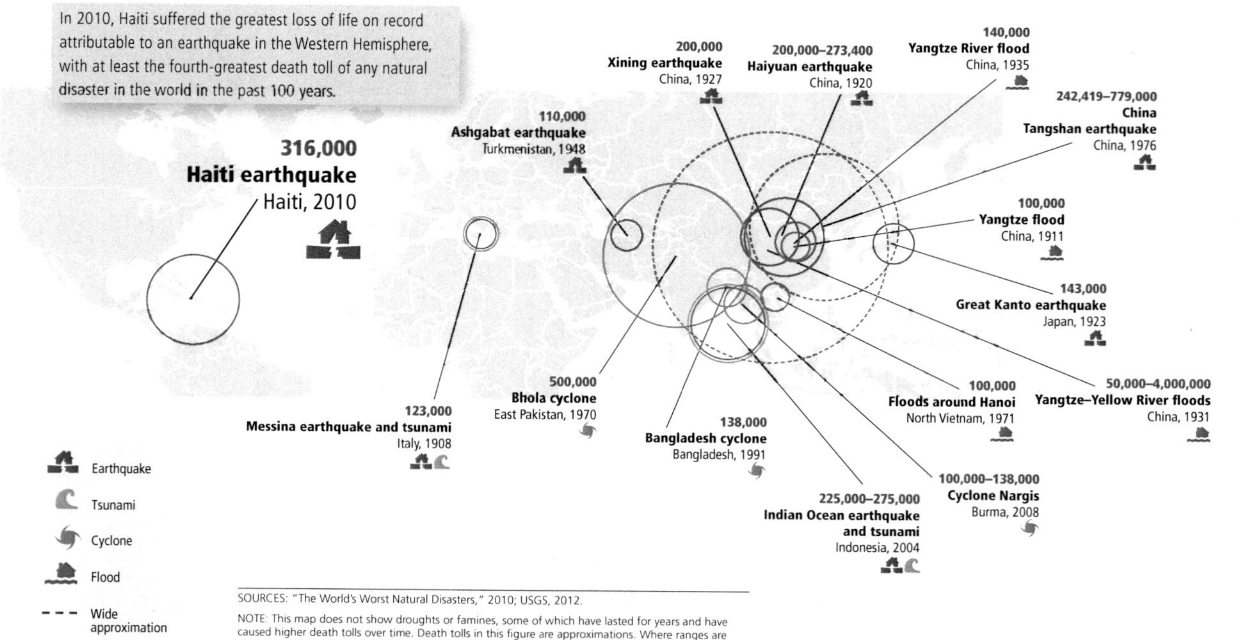

SOURCES: "The World's Worst Natural Disasters," 2010; USGS, 2012.

NOTE: This map does not show droughts or famines, some of which have lasted for years and have caused higher death tolls over time. Death tolls in this figure are approximations. Where ranges are shown, significantly different totals have been reported by different sources.

Base map: iStockphoto/Thinkstock

RAND *RR304-1.1*

The deputy commander of SOUTHCOM, LTG P. K. (Ken) Keen, was on a previously planned trip to Haiti and was in the residence of the U.S. ambassador when the earthquake struck. Given the fact that MINUSTAH, an established combined military organization, was already conducting security and stability operations in Haiti, U.S. and UN officials decided that, instead of establishing an additional combined joint task force (CJTF; sometimes also called a coalition joint task force) that might lead to confusion of roles and authorities or undermine MINUSTAH's credibility, it would be more effective to create a separate U.S. joint task force (JTF) to conduct humanitarian assistance (HA) and disaster relief (DR) efforts in coordination with MINUSTAH. Thus, JTF-Haiti would carry out Operation Unified Response. In the immediate aftermath of the earthquake, General Keen began requesting the deployment of U.S. military forces, including a headquarters element from the XVIII Airborne Corps, and he began to coordinate U.S. military relief efforts with the many other countries and relief organizations either already in Haiti or on their way. These efforts were part of what became the "largest international humanitarian response to a natural disaster in U.S. history."[3]

In addition to the widespread destruction and generally poor conditions that existed in Haiti before the earthquake, there were immediate challenges for the assistance and relief missions. The air and seaports had been destroyed, so responders had no way of delivering high volumes of much-needed relief supplies immediately after the disaster. A first priority of JTF-Haiti was to reopen the airport. Clearing and reopening the harbor at Port-au-Prince were also a high priority. The coordination required among so many well-meaning organizations to achieve these and the myriad other emergency response and relief tasks was daunting. In discussions between General Keen, the GoH, SOUTHCOM, and UN representatives in Haiti, it was agreed that MINUSTAH would continue its mission of providing security

---

[3] The U.S. government spent $1.5 billion on Haiti disaster relief by the end of 2010 and committed an additional $1.15 billion to be spent on reconstruction efforts through 2011. See U.S. Department of State, 2011a; U.S. Air Force, 2008; "Bush Aims to Boost US Tsunami Aid," 2005.

and stability in Haiti and that JTF-Haiti would focus on providing HA/DR.

The purpose of this study was to assess the effectiveness of JTF-Haiti, with the goal of informing the U.S. Army on how to best prepare for and support future HA/DR operations. This report describes how JTF-Haiti faced the aforementioned challenges, how it was organized, how it fit within the larger assistance and relief efforts, and how it measured its performance. The report concludes with some observations, findings, and recommendations to multiple levels of U.S. decisionmakers to inform their preparations for similar missions in the future.

Analytical Approach

This report employs process tracing to determine how JTF-Haiti was organized and how it executed its mission. It begins with a thorough review of the statutory authorities and policy directives that existed at the time of the earthquake to determine whether the available guidance was adequate to carry out such an operation. It then examines how JTF-Haiti fit into the whole-of-government approach, as well as the international response, in order to codify important lessons and identify ways in which the execution of similar future missions could be improved.

The report benefits from the many lessons-learned and after-action reports that have been produced by military, other-governmental, and nongovernmental organizations (NGOs).[4] The study team reviewed all of the reports that were available, as well as accounts in the peer-reviewed literature and media. We also received copies of the execute orders (EXORDs) for Operation Unified Response and daily situation reports and periodic command update briefings from military

[4] These included, for example, reports by SOUTHCOM, JTF-Haiti, Joint Center for Operational Analysis, U.S. Army South (ARSOUTH), Department of the Army Deputy Chief of Staff for Logistics (G-4), U.S. State Department, USAID, and the World Vision *Rapid Assessment Report: Haiti Earthquake Response* (Duryée, 2010).

units and other U.S. government agencies significantly participating in Operation Unified Response.[5]

With this base of knowledge, investigators then held semi-structured discussions with key participants in Operation Unified Response, including the JTF-Haiti commander and deputy commander (who became the second JTF-Haiti commander). We also consulted selected subordinate JTF-Haiti unit commanders and staff; DoD and Joint Staff participants; major supporting commands; DoD analytical organizations; subject-matter experts, including international aid organizations and academics; other U.S. government agencies, including USAID; foreign participants; and NGOs.

Once all of the information was gathered, the team reconstructed events surrounding the Haiti earthquake and assessed the U.S. military response. The team concluded its work with a series of observations, findings, and recommendations.

Report Organization

Chapter Two presents information on how the United States is organized to respond to foreign disasters and how the response to the Haiti earthquake differed from the typical approach. It describes the roles of U.S. governmental organizations, such as the Department of State and DoD, and it provides detailed descriptions of relevant parts of DoD that play roles in international response operations. It includes an analysis of the authorities that exist for DoD to participate in international response. Then it describes how the federal departments, agencies, and services were organized to execute the whole-of-government U.S. response that President Obama ordered for the Haiti earthquake.

Chapter Three documents the U.S. military response to the Haiti earthquake. It explains how JTF-Haiti was formed and how its forces were selected and deployed to Haiti. It further describes how JTF-Haiti

---

[5] These included, for example, SOUTHCOM, JTF-Haiti (including the Humanitarian Assistance Coordination Center [HACC]), XVIII Airborne Corps, U.S. State Department, and USAID.

was organized, how it executed its mission, and how it evolved over time. It also presents how JTF-Haiti interacted with and supported the many other organizations involved in the relief effort. It concludes with observations about JTF-Haiti's accomplishments and some of the problems it encountered. Chapter Four presents study conclusions and recommendations.

A Note About Terminology

Our research indicates that various authorities, policy documents, reports, and statements from relevant U.S. government agencies use a variety of terms to describe the activities covered in this report. Some use *disaster relief* as an overarching term that also includes humanitarian assistance. Others use *humanitarian assistance* as the inclusive term. Some use both. For this report, we use the collective term *humanitarian assistance and disaster relief* (HA/DR) to cover the full range of response to both natural and manmade incidents, including major environmental events.

CHAPTER TWO

National Organization and Response

This chapter provides some background information needed to understand the U.S. military's role in Operation Unified Response. First, it explains how the United States is organized to provide HA/DR in foreign countries. Then it describes how the nation responded to the Haiti earthquake.

How the United States Is Organized to Provide Foreign Humanitarian Assistance and Disaster Relief

This section describes various presidential documents covering foreign HA/DR and explains the authorities and organizational structures of the principal departments and agencies of the federal government that provide foreign HA/DR—namely, the U.S. Department of State, USAID, and DoD and its components with responsibilities in this arena.[1] For purposes of this chapter, the term *authorities* refers to specific constitutional, statutory, or other legal authorities to engage in such missions. Particularly for DoD, this section also describes certain implementing policy directives and instructions.

---

[1] Depending on the circumstances that requires U.S. HA/DR, other U.S. departments and agencies may be involved in a particular mission (e.g., the Department of Agriculture, Department of Health and Human Services, Department of the Treasury).

U.S. Department of State

The Secretary of State (SECSTATE) has the long-standing, preeminent authority to manage the foreign affairs of the United States. Indeed, tracing its roots directly back to the earliest statutes of the Republic, the secretary is empowered to conduct and manage, on behalf of the President, all manner of foreign relations and intercourse.[2]

Both by statute and by executive order, SECSTATE is authorized and empowered to conduct exclusively most programs for foreign assistance, including most provisions of the Foreign Assistance Act of 1961 (Pub. L. 87-195), as amended (Title 22 U.S. Code § 2151 et seq.). Specifically, the provisions of 22 U.S. Code § 2292—authorizing the President to furnish foreign DR—were delegated to SECSTATE by Executive Order 12163 (Carter, 1979).

Within the State Department, the Director of the Office of U.S. Foreign Assistance (DFA) is the principal staff member for coordinating foreign assistance programs. Among the seven core areas in the DFA vision statement is "Respond to urgent humanitarian needs." The DFA mission statement includes integrating "foreign assistance planning and resource management across State and USAID" and allocating "State and USAID foreign assistance funding" (see U.S. Department of State, undated).

The State Department expends significant sums on international DR. The fiscal year (FY) 2011 estimate is $845 million, with an FY 2012 budget request for $860 million (U.S. Department of State, 2011b).[3]

U.S. Agency for International Development

USAID is an independent federal government agency and is "the principal U.S. agency to extend assistance to countries recovering from disaster, trying to escape poverty, and engaging in democratic reforms" ("U.S. Agency for International Development," 2013).

---

[2] Title 22 U.S. Code § 2656, first recorded in nearly identical form in legislation in 1789.

[3] The actual expenditures for FY 2010 were $1.305 billion, reflecting base appropriations plus additional funding from two supplemental appropriation acts. These figures do not reflect significant contributions to international organizations that are also involved in DR.

USAID policy documents acknowledge that it receives "overall foreign policy *guidance*" from the Secretary of State (emphasis added) (See, e.g., USAID, date unknown). Nevertheless, a section of Title 22 of the U.S. Code is significantly more explicit:

> Sec. 6592. Administrator of AID reporting to Secretary of State. The Administrator of the Agency for International Development, appointed pursuant to section 2384(a) of this title, shall report to and be under the direct authority and foreign policy guidance of the Secretary of State.

Notwithstanding this section and the delegations of authority to SECSTATE, the President has, pursuant to § 493 of the Foreign Assistance Act, designated the USAID administrator as the President's Special Coordinator for International Disaster Assistance (see, e.g., W. Clinton, 1995).

To help establish a common vision, establish priorities, ensure unity of effort, and avoid major policy disagreements, the State Department and USAID periodically publish a joint strategic plan.[4]

In practice, USAID is the main U.S. government agency for *administering* the major portion of U.S. foreign assistance, including key programs authorized by the Foreign Assistance Act of 1961. To do so, it is organized both regionally and functionally (see USAID, 2013a).

To accomplish its work, USAID frequently partners with private voluntary organizations, academia, business entities, and international organizations, and it often coordinates directly with foreign government agencies and with U.S. government organizations, including DoD (for which, see further discussion in Chapter Three). USAID has personnel detailed to most U.S. embassies around the world.

Office of U.S. Foreign Disaster Assistance

Located within the USAID Bureau for Democracy, Conflict, and Humanitarian Assistance (DCHA), the Office of U.S. Foreign Disaster Assistance (OFDA) is the principal entity "for facilitating and coor-

---

4 The current version, for FYs 2007–2012, is U.S. Department of State and USAID, 2007.

dinating U.S. Government emergency assistance overseas . . . to save lives, alleviate human suffering, and reduce the social and economic impact of humanitarian emergencies worldwide." OFDA coordinates response not only to all forms of natural disasters but also for emergencies involving "civil conflict, acts of terrorism, or industrial accidents" (see USAID, 2013b).

Disaster Assistance Response Team

OFDA may deploy a disaster assistance response team (DART) into the disaster area to assist in the coordination of the DR effort. A DART provides specialists, trained in a variety of skills, to assist U.S. embassies and USAID missions with the management of the U.S. government response to a foreign disaster. Its composition and specific mission will depend on the nature, severity, and duration of a particular disaster. (The DART will also work closely with the U.S. military when it is participating in foreign DR operations. See further discussion in Chapter Three.)

The DART operates in five functional areas:

- management
- operations
- planning
- logistics
- administration.

Depending on the scope of the disaster and composition of the team, the DART is capable of

- making assessments
- recommending response activities
- managing relief activities
- coordinating distribution of relief and supplies
- liaison with government officials and NGOs.[5]

---

[5] For more-detailed information on the DART, see USAID, 2005, Chapter Four.

Response Management Team

In certain circumstances, the OFDA director may establish a response management team (RMT). The RMT serves as the primary liaison between USAID headquarters and the foreign response operations. It is the USAID principal point of contact with the DART, oversees headquarters-based support to field operations, and is the USAID representative for working-level interagency coordination (USAID, 2005, p. IV-13 et seq.).

U.S. Department of Defense

This subsection describes the principal authorities, policies, and basic organizational structures of the components of DoD for conducting foreign HA/DR operations. DoD agreements with other U.S. government agencies and organizational structures for a specific disaster (including Operation Unified Response for Haiti) are discussed later in this report.

Authorities Generally

There is ample statutory authority for components of DoD to provide a wide range of HA/DR.

U.S. Code Title 10 § 404 is the basic authority for DoD to provide such assistance, at the request or agreement of a foreign government and as directed by the President, for both natural and manmade disasters, "when necessary to prevent loss of lives or serious harm to the environment." Assistance may include transportation, supplies, services, and equipment.[6] DoD receives annual authorization and appropriations for such much of that assistance through the Overseas Humanitarian Disaster and Civic Aid (OHDACA) program accounts.

A presidential executive order provides further implementation instructions for assistance under § 404. In Executive Order 12966 (W. Clinton, 1995), the President directed the Secretary of Defense (SecDef) to provide assistance under that section only

---

[6] Paragraph (e) of that section limits the provision of DoD transportation to those situations in which "other sources to provide such transportation are not readily available."

> at the direction of the President; or with the concurrence of the Secretary of State; or in emergency situations in order to save human lives, where there is not sufficient time to seek the prior initial concurrence of the Secretary of State, in which case the Secretary of Defense shall advise, and seek the concurrence of, the Secretary of State as soon as practicable thereafter.

The authority under § 404 is to be distinguished materially from that contained in 10 U.S.C. § 401. In § 401, SecDef is authorized to provide humanitarian and civic assistance "in conjunction with authorized military operations." Limitations on that authority include determinations by the secretary that such assistance will promote "the security interests of the United States and the country in which the activities are to be carried out" and "the specific operational skills of the members of the armed forces" performing the assistance.[7]

In addition to the foregoing, DoD is authorized under 10 U.S.C. § 402, to transport without charge—but only on a "space-available" basis—humanitarian supplies provided by nongovernmental entities. Activities under this program—known as the Denton Program, after its sponsor, then–U.S. Senator Jeremiah Denton (Alabama)—requires determinations by SecDef that such activity is consistent with U.S. foreign policy; that the supplies are "suitable" and "usable"; that they will, in fact, be used for humanitarian purposes; and that adequate distribution is available.[8]

Additionally, 10 U.S.C. § 2557 authorizes SecDef to make available to SECSTATE certain nonlethal excess DoD supplies for foreign humanitarian purposes. And § 2561 authorizes SecDef to expend DoD funds appropriated for HA to provide DoD transportation assistance and for other humanitarian purposes worldwide. That section

---

[7] Additional conditions include a provision that the assistance "complement, and may not duplicate" other social and economic assistance provided by the U.S. government to that country; and such assistance may not be provided "(directly or indirectly) to any individual, group, or organization engaged in military or paramilitary activity." Moreover, assistance may not be provided under this section unless SECSTATE approves.

[8] There are also restrictions similar to ones contained in §§ 401 and 404 that prohibit distribution to those engaged in military or paramilitary activities and in situations in which other transportation is not readily available.

also authorizes SecDef to use his or her authority to transport supplies for an event that "threatens serious harm to the environment," but only if other transportation sources are not readily available. In this latter case of environmental incidents, SecDef may seek reimbursement from a requesting agency for DoD costs incurred in the activity.

Although many DoD HA/DR activities are funded by specific appropriations (e.g., OHDACA funds), SecDef may, if such funding is not available for the intended purpose or has previously been expended, also seek reimbursement from a requesting agency under the provisions of what is commonly called the Economy Act (31 U.S.C. § 1535).

Office of the Secretary of Defense Implementing Policies

The oft-cited[9] principal Office of the Secretary of Defense (OSD) policy directive for DoD HA/DR is DoD Directive (DoDD) 5100.46, *Foreign Disaster Relief* (Office of the Deputy Secretary of State, 2012). It provides general direction to entities in OSD, the military departments, "the Organization of the Joint Chiefs of Staff, the Defense Agencies, and the Unified and Specified Commands" [sic].[10] It provides limited information on the various forms of HA/DR activities that the department can perform. Significantly, the version in effect at the time of the Haiti earthquake was dated December 4, 1975, and had not been republished, amended, or updated before relief efforts in Haiti began. As a result, the version in effect cited none of the foregoing specific Title 10 sections authorizing such DoD activities because all were enacted subsequent to the publication of this DoDD and Title 10 has been amended numerous times since enactment. The DoDD likewise did not cite Executive Order 12163 (Carter, 1979) on delegation of Foreign Assistance Act authorities and, significantly, Executive Order 12966 on DoD foreign DR under § 404.

Less significant—but nevertheless material—is the fact that the 1975 version of DoDD 5100.46 referred to several obsolete organizations within DoD and one in the Department of State.

---

[9] Including in the executive orders and operation orders for Operation Unified Response.

[10] This discussion refers to the 1975 DoDD, which was in force during the response to the Haiti earthquake, and it has since been revised.

By contrast, other similar DoD directives and instructions are significantly more current. Examples include DoD Instruction (DoDI) 2205.02, *Humanitarian and Civic Assistance (HCA) Activities* (Office of the Under Secretary of Defense for Policy, 2008) (which covers only instructions related to the provisions of § 401 above); DoDI 3000.05, *Stability Operations* (Office of the Under Secretary of Defense for Policy, 2009) (which covers certain general aspects of foreign humanitarian relief and assistance); DoDI 6000.16, *Military Health Support for Stability Operations* (Office of the Under Secretary of Defense for Personnel and Readiness, 2010) (which covers discrete health matters in stability operations that may include foreign HA/DR); and DoDI 2000.21, *Foreign Consequence Management (FCM)* (Office of the Under Secretary of Defense for Policy, 2006) (which covers DoD response to foreign chemical, biological, radiological, nuclear, or high-yield explosive [CBRNE] incidents).

Similarly, related joint doctrine is significantly more current than DoDD 5100.46. Joint Publication (JP) 3-29, *Foreign Humanitarian Assistance*, which covers the full range of DoD HA/DR activities—and more—is dated March 17, 2009 (Joint Chiefs of Staff, 2009).

Creating a current, comprehensive directive to replace DoDD 5100.46 could potentially go a long way toward alleviating some of the issues raised in various U.S. Government Accountability Office (GAO) and Congressional Research Service reports to Congress, which assess DoD involvement in HA/DR operations (including one specific to SOUTHCOM operations in Haiti) (Kelley, 1993; Pendleton, 2010; Serafino, 2008). Issues include

- comprehensive procedures for reporting the level and full costs for HA/DR
- procedures for ensuring that such activities meet U.S. foreign policy objectives and host-country needs
- processes for independent evaluations of COCOM activities in this area
- methods for ensuring that such activities promote military skills

- adequate organizational structures, planning, and exercises within COCOMs to enable effective response to major incidents requiring DoD support for HA/DR
- relationships between military and NGOs
- potential disadvantages of using military versus civilian entities for such assistance
- adequate procedures for effective coordination between DoD and other U.S. government entities, NGOs, international organizations, and host-nation and coalition entities for these activities.

In addition, a complete revision of or replacement for DoDD 5100.46 could also provide current and definitive guidance on such activities to all DoD components.

Office of the Secretary of Defense and Defense Agency Organizations

Policy direction and oversight within OSD for HA/DR activities had previously been handled in the Office of the Assistant Secretary for International Security Affairs. Following recent reorganization in OSD, these matters are now handled in the Office of the Assistant Secretary of Defense for Special Operations/Low-Intensity Conflict by the Deputy Assistant Secretary of Defense for Partnership Strategy and Stability Operations.

The Defense Security Cooperation Agency (DSCA) is the DoD entity primarily responsible for administering most of the department's international security cooperation programs. Within DSCA, the Office of Humanitarian Assistance, Disaster Relief, and Mine Action is responsible for providing program management for DoD HA programs funded with the OHDACA appropriations for all geographic COCOMs. DSCA manages the funding and activities for virtually all the programs authorized in the various statutory provisions described above. It coordinates management of these DoD programs within DoD entities and with other agencies of the U.S. government, especially the Department of State and USAID (see DSCA, 2013).

Chairman, Joint Chiefs of Staff, and the Joint Staff Organizations

The Chairman of the Joint Chiefs of Staff (CJCS) is the principal military adviser to the President and SecDef. As such, he advises the National Command Authority on military operations, including those involving HA/DR. In that position, he also communicates relevant orders of the National Command Authority to the various combatant commanders (DoD, 2010).

Within the Joint Staff, the Director for Operational Plans and Joint Force Development (J-7) is primarily responsible for reviewing and recommending to the CJCS the approval of operation plans in support of foreign HA/DR. The Director for Operations (J-3) recommends to the CJCS the form and substance of EXORDs for such activities. The Director for Logistics (J-4) provides oversight of supporting joint logistics operations for such activities (JP 3-29, p. II-7).

Combatant Command Organizations

Geographic combatant commanders (GCCs) have wide latitude in the way they organize to conduct HA/DR activities, both pre-event and during actual operations. Commanders historically have created some form of JTF for such operations, structuring and resourcing it to conduct operations most effectively (JP 3-29, p. II-7).

Some commanders also have the availability of a Standing Joint Force Headquarters (SJFHQ) around which to form, through augmentation, a JTF, or conversely by using core elements of the SJFHQ as augmentation to a JTF created for a particular operation. Around the time that Operation Unified Response occurred, however, proposals to remove SJFHQ structures from the geographic commands were being discussed, and, in May 2011, USNORTHCOM disestablished its SJFHQ, perhaps in anticipation of an imminent change to that effect in the Unified Command Plan (see Doscher, 2011). Yet SOUTHCOM had an SJFHQ available at the time of the Haiti earthquake and, as did USPACOM, continued to show it in its organizational structure in 2011 (see Doscher, 2011, and USPACOM, undated).

In addition to a JTF—and, in most cases, prior to its deployment and full operational capability—the commander has the option of forming other entities to assist in the COCOM mission. They may include the following:

- crisis action team for immediate deployment and assessment of the situation
- HA survey team (HAST) to provide assessment of host nations' capabilities and facilities; determine points of contact with other governmental and nongovernmental entities involved; and coordinate arrangements for initial delivery of supplies, equipment, and personnel
- HACC to assist initially with interagency coordination (until other organizations are formed to perform those functions) (JP 3-29, p. II-8).

Army Organizations

The Department of the Army provides traditional Title 10 support for Army units involved in any military operation, including HA/DR. Research for this report did not indicate any Pentagon-level Army organization with a specific responsibility for such activities.

Within the geographic COCOMs, the Army Component Command is generally responsible for Army support to contingency operations, including foreign HA/DR. Responsibilities include force provision; logistics, engineer, medical, and other mission support; and capabilities for command and control (including for joint or combined headquarters). Examples of such commands include ARSOUTH and U.S. Army Pacific. In many such operations, Army units have provided the greatest proportion of total military personnel on the ground dedicated to foreign HA or DR missions.

Interagency Organizations

The National Security Council

The National Security Council (NSC) serves as the President's principal entity for coordinating policy among various government agencies (White House, undated). Within the NSC structure, various organizations may be involved in considering important policy issues and eventually recommending to the President a particular course of action. A

Principals Committee—essentially the full NSC without the President or Vice President—historically has met to discuss important national security issues and to review and coordinate specific policy recommendations developed by subordinate NSC organizations. The Deputies Committee—normally composed of cabinet and independent agency deputies—is the next level down for the consideration of policy issues affecting the interagency (Obama, 2009).

NSC Interagency Policy Committees (at times called Policy Coordinating Committees [PCCs]) are responsible for the "[m]anagement and development of national security policies by multiple agencies of the United States Government" (Obama, 2009). Traditionally, there has been a PCC for International Development and Humanitarian Assistance, chaired by the President's Special Coordinator for International Disaster Assistance (who is also the administrator of USAID), to consider policy matters involving foreign HA/DR (JP 3-29, p. II-2).

Organizational Relationships

JP 3-29 graphically depicts the typical interagency coordination relationships that may take place during actual HA or DR operations (see Figure 2.1).

JP 3-29 also depicts the basic information flow among interagency entities when OFDA and DoD are both involved in HA/DR operations (see Figure 2.2).

The next section will compares the "typical" organizational structures and relationships described above with those actually put in place for Operation Unified Response for Haiti.

How the United States Responded to the Haiti Earthquake

The levels of damage and human suffering wrought by this disaster both complicated U.S. efforts to render HA and added to their urgency. Already one of the world's poorest countries before the earthquake, the disaster decapitated Haiti's government and temporarily incapacitated MINUSTAH and the many NGOs that were already present

Figure 2.1
Interagency Coordination for Foreign Humanitarian Assistance

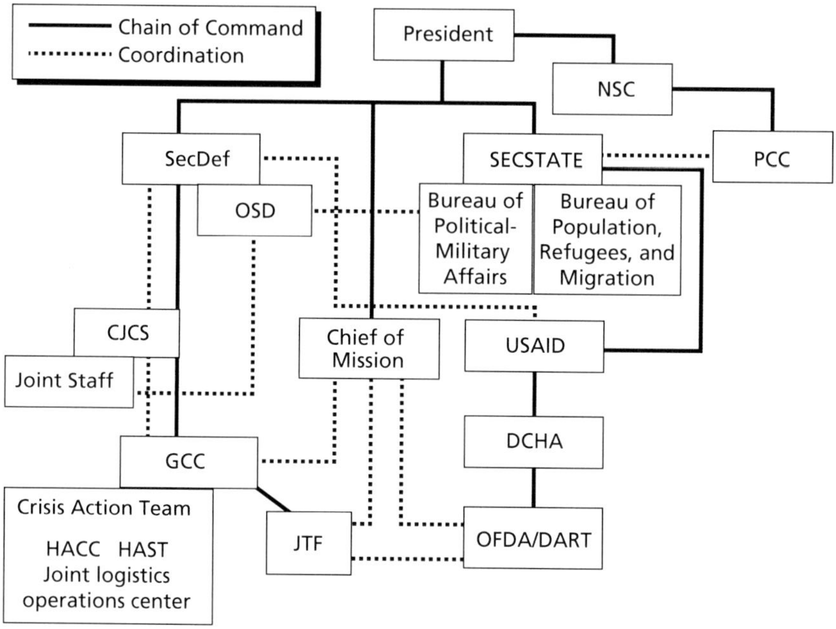

RAND *RR304-2.1*

and providing support on an ongoing basis. As previously stated, the event destroyed 14 of the country's 16 government ministry buildings, the presidential palace, and the parliament building, as well as the MINUSTAH headquarters building. Power was out throughout Haiti's capital, Port-au-Prince. Extensive damage rendered the airport and harbor inoperable. City streets and nearby roads were choked with rubble, making them impassible to vehicular traffic (Margesson and Taft-Morales, 2010, pp. 1–2; also see Keen, Floriano Piexoto, et al., 2010, pp. 2, 7).

These conditions made it difficult for the GoH to even convey a request for international assistance. Fortunately, the residence of U.S. Ambassador to Haiti Kenneth H. Merten survived the earthquake, and SOUTHCOM deputy commander LTG P. K. (Ken) Keen was there visiting the ambassador at 4:53 p.m. on January 12 when the

Figure 2.2
Interagency Coordination Flow

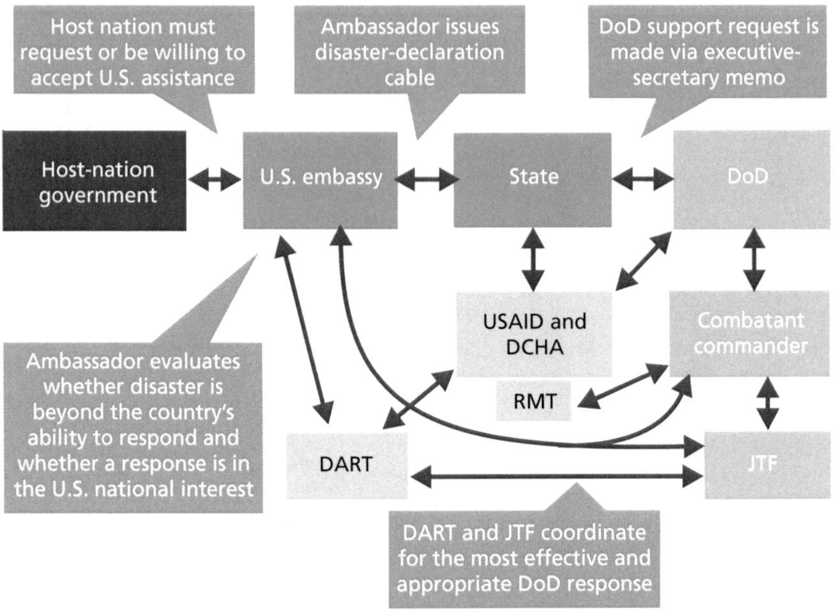

NOTE: Gray boxes indicate DCHA and DoD responses.
RAND *RR304-2.2*

quake occurred. Shortly after the event, a GoH representative rode up on a motorbike and delivered an oral request for U.S. assistance, which Ambassador Merten relayed to the U.S. government and General Keen relayed to SOUTHCOM.[11]

President Obama immediately pledged U.S. support, and SECSTATE Hillary Clinton announced that the United States would provide military and civilian DR to affected families. On January 13, President Obama designated USAID as lead federal agency for coordinating the U.S. response. Ambassador Merten declared Haiti a disaster area, clearing the way for OFDA to provide an initial $50,000 of aid through the U.S. embassy (USAID, 2010b). On January 14, the

[11] Discussion between LTG P. K. Keen and RAND researchers Gary Cecchine and Forrest Morgan on April 20, 2010 (hereafter referred to as *Keen discussion*).

Obama administration announced that it would make $100 million available to meet DR needs (Margesson and Taft-Morales, 2010, p. 14). That same day, the CJCS issued an EXORD authorizing U.S. military forces to commence Operation Unified Response, providing HA/DR to earthquake victims in Haiti. With SecDef approval, SOUTHCOM stood up JTF-Haiti and appointed General Keen as its commander to lead DoD relief efforts in country.

As previously mentioned, OFDA is an office within DCHA. Historically, OFDA has managed HA to foreign disasters by sending a DART to the scene and assembling an RMT in Washington to coordinate interagency support. Those actions were taken in this case as well. OFDA stood up an RMT on the evening of January 12 and deployed a DART, the first seven members of which arrived at 4:15 p.m. on January 13 (USAID, 2010b). However, given the magnitude and urgency of the disaster, President Obama ordered a "whole-of-government" approach, requiring multiple federal departments and agencies to "launch a swift, coordinated and aggressive effort to save lives and support the recovery in Haiti" (White House, 2010).[12] Consequently, an interagency task force was assembled in Washington, and a newly created entity, the USAID Office of the Response Coordinator (ORC), was stood up in Haiti to coordinate efforts on the ground. This created parallel lines of authority between these entities and the RMT and DART and led to some confusion in the field regarding roles and responsibilities vis-à-vis the DART and ORC. Over the course of the relief effort, roles evolved, with the DART's responsibilities diminishing and the RMT's scope shrinking accordingly because it provided interagency support to the DART alone, versus the Interagency Task Force's responsibility for supporting the entire relief effort (Guha-Sapir et al., 2010, p. 28).

Because of the magnitude of the disaster and the whole-of-government approach chosen to respond to it, a much broader array of

---

[12] The whole-of-government concept was adopted from recommendations made in the final report of the 2008 Project on National Security Reform. That study focused on ways to improve interagency coordination for more-effective security of the U.S. homeland. The U.S. response to the Haiti earthquake was the first time it was employed. See Project on National Security Reform, 2008.

federal departments and agencies participated in this relief effort than in previous foreign disasters. Figure 2.3 depicts the many government organizations involved in the U.S. response to the Haiti earthquake,

Figure 2.3
U.S. Organizations That Supported Relief Efforts in Haiti

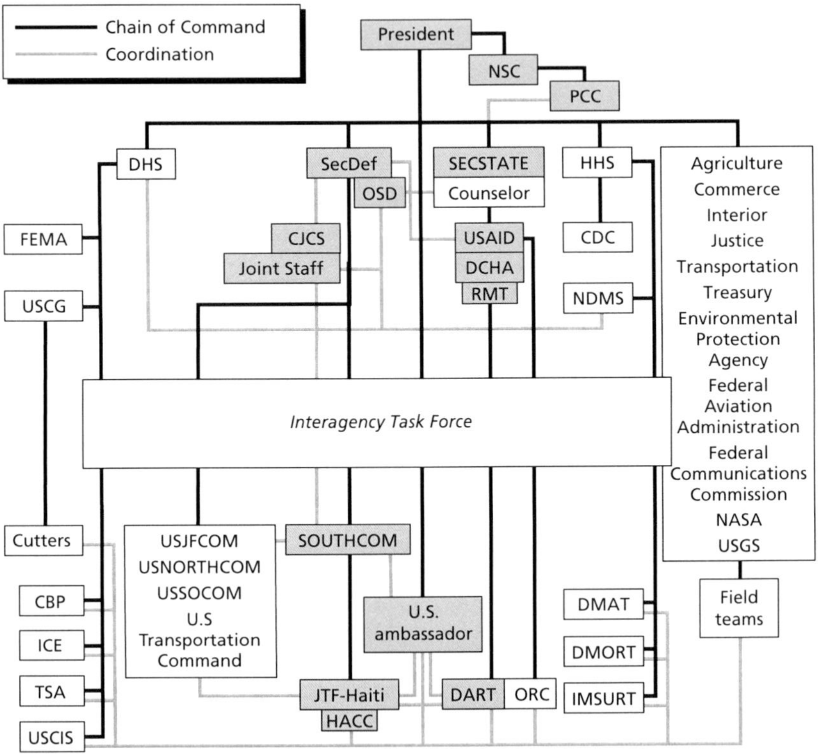

NOTE: Orange boxes indicate those typically involved in U.S. responses to major foreign disasters. White boxes indicate the additional departments, agencies, and military commands that played significant roles in supporting HA/DR operations in Haiti. HHS = U.S. Department of Health and Human Services. NASA = National Aeronautics and Space Administration. FEMA = Federal Emergency Management Agency. NDMS = National Disaster Medical System. USCG = U.S. Coast Guard. CBP = U.S. Customs and Border Protection. ICE = U.S. Immigration and Customs Enforcement. TSA = Transportation Security Administration. USCIS = U.S. Citizenship and Immigration Services. USJFCOM = U.S. Joint Forces Command. USNORTHCOM = U.S. Northern Command. USSOCOM = U.S. Special Operations Command. DMAT = disaster medical assistance team. DMORT = disaster mortuary operational response team. IMSURT = International Medical Surgical Response Team.

RAND *RR304-2.3*

and it shows the relationships between them. The individuals and organizations shown in the orange boxes are those typically involved in U.S. responses to major foreign disasters. Those shown in the white boxes are the additional departments, agencies, and military commands that played significant roles in supporting HA/DR operations in Haiti.

Authority to provide U.S. assistance to foreign governments in response to natural or manmade disasters is, by law, vested in the President. When the Haiti earthquake occurred, "the White House and the Department of State took special interest in the response from the beginning, playing large roles in the coordination, planning and execution" (Guha-Sapir et al., 2010, p. 25). The Principals Committee and Deputies Committee of the NSC directed strategic planning and policy development, with assistance from the NSC's PCC. During the first two days of the response, NSC principals and deputies met daily at the White House, but, by day three, it was clear that video teleconferences (VTCs) would have to be established to coordinate interagency functions and allow key individuals to interact from separate locations. DoD was instrumental in setting up the VTCs. Led by senior State Department officials, they were conducted at least twice daily from mid-January to mid-February, after which they occurred less frequently (Guha-Sapir et al., 2010, pp. 29–30).

As the federal department responsible for foreign affairs, State plays a central role in any U.S. response to a foreign disaster. When the Haiti earthquake occurred, Secretary Clinton appointed counselor and chief of staff Cheryl Mills to lead the response for the department, instead of the chief of the Bureau of Western Hemisphere Affairs, as might normally be the case. Mills had been working on a long-term development strategy for Haiti during the prior 12 months and was familiar with the Haitian government and its key institutions. Among the first actions State officials took were to open an emergency operations center for round-the-clock operations and stand up six separate task forces to accomplish such functions as evacuating the 16,800 U.S. citizens then in Haiti; processing visa applications for Haitian refugees wanting to come to the United States; planning for recovery, reconstruction, and stabilization; and working with the U.S. Department of Homeland Security (DHS) and the American and International

Red Cross to locate and assist orphans and vulnerable minors (Doerge, 2010, p. 15).

Two other offices in the State Department key to the relief effort (not depicted in Figure 2.3) were the Office of U.S. Foreign Assistance, which coordinated activities with USAID and gave departmental approval for the necessary spending, and the office of the Under Secretary for Management, which coordinated resource requirements and submitted Haiti relief funding requests to Congress and the Office of Management and Budget (Guha-Sapir et al., 2010, p. 40).

Although DHS has primary responsibility for securing the U.S. homeland and responding to disasters in the United States, it too provided important support to the Haiti relief operation. USCG was among the first responders, sending six cutters to Haitian waters. The first, U.S. Coast Guard Cutter (USCGC) *Forward*, arrived at Port-au-Prince on January 13, where its crew conducted an initial assessment and began rendering immediate aid ("First U.S. Vessel Arrives at Port-au-Prince," 2010). USCG later assisted in air-medical evacuations of injured U.S. civilian personnel, opening Haiti's ports and coordinating the arrival of seaborne relief supplies (Margesson and Taft-Morales, 2010, p. 15).

FEMA, a part of DHS since 2003, is responsible for managing response operations for disasters occurring in the United States, but it too played an important role in the Haiti relief effort. FEMA activated its National Response Coordination Center (NRCC) at level II operations, and the FEMA administrator co-led the Interagency Task Force with the USAID administrator.[13] FEMA set up an incident support base in Florida to facilitate the transport of supplies to Haiti and, by January 16, had deployed an incident response team and ten domestic urban search-and-rescue (USAR) teams in Haiti (FEMA, 2010).

DHS's CBP, ICE, TSA, and USCIS all contributed to Haiti relief efforts. CBP deployed 122 border-protection officers and 25 agricultural

---

[13] The NRCC is activated at one of three levels of operation: level I (full activation), level II (midlevel activation), and level III (minimum activation). Level I activation includes a recall of representatives from all 15 Emergency Support Functions (ESFs). Level II and III activations typically involve recalls of selected ESFs, tailored to the needs of the DR. See FEMA, undated.

specialists to Miami for facilitating the movement of people from Haiti to the United States and foreign-government assets through the United States to Haiti (Guha-Sapir et al., 2010, p. 52). ICE agents deployed to Santo Domingo, Dominican Republic, and to Port-au-Prince. They and CBP provided security for supply convoys and evacuees moving between those cities and helped move adopted children from the U.S. embassy to the Port-au-Prince airport (CBP, 2010). The ICE Office of Intelligence also helped Haitian authorities identify escaped criminals after the jail in Port-au-Prince collapsed. TSA deployed officers to Haiti to provide security for U.S. citizens evacuating the country and technical assistance to airport personnel to facilitate the rapid resumption of commercial air service to and from Port-au-Prince. USCIS helped establish procedures that allowed 1,100 children approved for humanitarian parole to come to the United States. USCIS also processed more than 43,000 applications from Haitian nationals seeking entry into the United States in Temporary Protected Status (Guha-Sapir et al., 2010, pp. 52–53).

HHS contributed to the Haiti earthquake response in five important ways. First, on January 13, it activated NDMS—a partnership between HHS, DoD, and DHS—and began deploying DMATs, DMORTs, and IMSURTs to Haiti within days of the quake. Second, because of the lack of medical facilities in Haiti and limited space on hospital ships deployed to the region, starting on February 1, 2010, HHS began using NDMS to fund U.S. hospitals to provide care to Haitian patients evacuated there with life-threatening injuries due to the earthquake (USAID, 2010c). Third, HHS helped coordinate and screen U.S. citizens volunteering to lend medical assistance in Haiti. Fourth, HHS worked with DHS and the State Department to provide services for orphans and other refugees coming into the United States. And fifth, throughout these activities, the Centers for Disease Control and Prevention (CDC) worked with Haiti's Ministry of Health to augment the existing human immunodeficiency virus/acquired immunodeficiency syndrome sentinel points so they could track the spread of other infectious diseases. Working with the Ministry of Health and USAID, the CDC also implemented a vaccination program that inoculated more than 2 million Haitian citizens (CDC, 2010; Guha-Sapir et al., 2010, pp. 54–55).

A host of other U.S. federal departments and agencies supported relief efforts in Haiti. When the RMT and Interagency Task Force were formed, the Departments of Agriculture, Commerce, Interior, Justice, Treasury, and Transportation all sent representatives to one or both, as did many subordinate and independent agencies, such as USGS and NASA. Many of these organizations provided support from their bases in the United States; several sent teams or representatives to Haiti, providing support but also adding to the logistical burden of the relief operation (see, for example, Eberhard et al., 2010; Jet Propulsion Laboratory, 2010). No other department, however, matched the level of support provided by DoD in terms of personnel and resources committed to the effort.

DoD has well-established relationships with the State Department and USAID—especially OFDA—for supporting relief efforts following foreign disasters.[14] DoD has capabilities to provide security, logistics, transportation, and analysis, in measures not available elsewhere in the federal system, which OFDA coordinates to support the humanitarian response.[15] Because Haiti and MINUSTAH were initially incapacitated by the earthquake, the U.S. military played a much greater role than usual in the initial response and continued to have extensive involvement in the recovery phase of the operation. Moreover, long-standing procedures for approving and then providing that support were abridged to streamline the process and get relief to disaster victims as quickly as possible. Because of the catastrophic nature of the disaster and the President's direction to rush U.S. assistance to the scene, the USAID administrator cleared DoD to take whatever action it felt was necessary before receiving specific direction to do so (Guha-Sapir et al., 2010, p. 43).

As commander of JTF-Haiti, General Keen used that request from USAID to get as much aid and assistance as possible to the people

---

[14] For details on this relationship, see Perry and Travayiakis, 2008.

[15] However, unlike in some past foreign DR missions, providing security was specifically not included in DoD's mission in Haiti (Keen discussion).

of Haiti, as quickly as possible. Chapter Three details the U.S. military response to the Haiti earthquake.

CHAPTER THREE

The Military Response to the Haiti Earthquake

The response to the 2010 Haiti earthquake was the U.S. military's largest international humanitarian effort in history. This was one of the most catastrophic natural disasters ever to befall a state in the Western Hemisphere. The suffering it created prompted countries and organizations from all over the world to render assistance to the GoH and Haiti's citizens. The United States was but one participant in this enormous effort, and DoD was but one element in Washington's whole-of-government response. That said, the U.S. military was the single-largest contributor in terms of personnel and other capabilities. The U.S. Army, in turn, played a key role in providing the forces and functional expertise that enabled JTF-Haiti and the international effort to save thousands of lives and attend to the suffering of those who survived the earthquake.

This chapter documents the U.S. military response to the Haiti earthquake. It explains how JTF-Haiti was formed and how its forces were selected and deployed to Haiti. It further describes how JTF-Haiti was organized, how it executed its mission, and how its responsibilities and force composition evolved over the three phases of Operation Unified Response. Then the chapter takes a closer look at how JTF-Haiti interacted with and supported the many other organizations involved in the relief effort. Finally, the chapter concludes with some observations about JTF-Haiti's accomplishments and some of the problems it encountered.

Establishing Joint Task Force–Haiti

From Warning Order to Joint Operation

Within hours of the earthquake, DoD sent a warning order (WARNORD) to SOUTHCOM and supporting organizations to prepare forces for HA/DR operations in Haiti in support of USAID, the President's designated lead federal agency for the nation's overall response. That order prompted a series of immediate actions in SOUTHCOM and other military headquarters, such as initial requests for forces and for intelligence, surveillance, and reconnaissance (ISR) collection from assets over Haiti to assess the damage there. Figure 3.1 illustrates the many events that occurred during the next three days.

As Figure 3.1 indicates, many activities were set in motion before Operation Unified Response officially began on January 14, 2010. To implement the President's direction for a "swift and aggressive effort to save lives and support the recovery," the CJCS communicated the authority for SOUTHCOM to provide a task force to lead the military's response in Haiti. On January 13, 2010, SOUTHCOM established a joint force headquarters (JFHQ) in Port-au-Prince. That headquarters became the nucleus of JTF-Haiti the following day, when SecDef ordered Operation Unified Response to commence. Because SOUTHCOM deputy commander General Keen was already in Port-au-Prince and in contact with U.S. and Haitian officials, it was decided that he would command JTF-Haiti.

The mission of JTF-Haiti was stated as follows:

> JTF-Haiti conducts humanitarian assistance/foreign disaster response operations in support of USAID in Haiti to save lives, mitigate near-term human suffering and accelerate relief efforts to facilitate transition to GoH, UN, and USAID. (Keen, 2010b)

It is important to point out the implications of this mission statement. JTF-Haiti was not established to restore Haiti to its pre-earthquake condition; rather, its mission was to mitigate near-term suffering and accelerate relief efforts. The goal was to turn over control of the relief effort to USAID and the United Nations and return national administration to the GoH as soon as possible.

Figure 3.1
Operation Unified Response Timeline, January 12–15, 2010

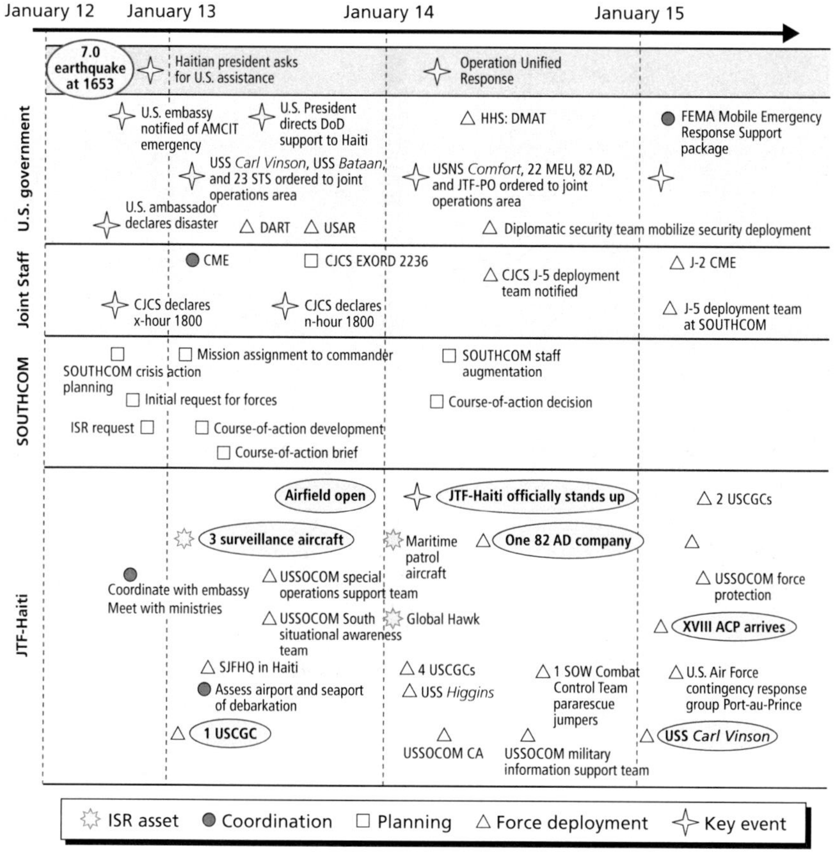

SOURCE: Keen, 2010b.
NOTE: AMCIT = U.S. citizen. USNS = U.S. Navy ship. AD = airborne division. STS = special tactics squadron. MEU = marine expeditionary unit. JTF-PO = JTF–Port Opening. x-hour = time of WARNORD. CME = crisis-management element. n-hour = time of notification. J-5 = Director for Strategic Plans and Policy. J-2 = Director for Intelligence. SOW = special operations wing. CA = civil affairs. ACP = assault command post.
RAND *RR304-3.1*

Requirements Assessment and Force Selection

A formal process exists within DoD for determining requirements and tailoring forces when called upon to provide HA/DR support to USAID and foreign governments. When the request is received from USAID and support is ordered by SecDef, the responsible COCOM sends a HAST to the scene of the disaster to assess the level and nature of support needed. The HAST then submits a report for COCOM commander review. With the commander's approval, the COCOM publishes orders to subordinate forces and requests whatever support is needed from other organizations. That process was not employed at the beginning of Operation Unified Response.

Because of the magnitude of the disaster and the urgent need to provide assistance as soon as possible, no formal assessment was done before forces were set in motion. With limited communications and little information about conditions in the country following the earthquake, General Keen and SOUTHCOM initiated verbal orders of commanding officer (VOCOs) to enable requests for military forces to be expedited. General Keen then used the telephone at Ambassador Merten's residence and later at the U.S. embassy to establish a series of phone conferences with generals commanding units that had the capabilities that he felt would be needed.

General Keen applied his judgment as a senior military commander to assemble the capabilities and resources that he believed that he would need to accomplish the mission. Knowing that command and control of a major military response would be a serious challenge in the devastated country, he called the commander of U.S. Army's XVIII Airborne Corps and arranged for the deployment of its ACP.

Likewise, General Keen knew that the earthquake had closed the international airport at Port-au-Prince, a facility essential to the relief effort. The control tower had been put out of operation, and it was uncertain whether the runway was safe to use. General Keen arranged to have the Air Force Special Operations Command (AFSOC) 1 SOW send an Air Force STS to Haiti. It arrived 26 hours after the earthquake and reestablished flight operations 28 minutes after reaching the scene. The Air Force special operators managed air traffic control functions until control of the airport could be returned to Haitian authorities (Fraser and Hertzelle, 2010).

General Keen further assessed that the relief effort would need search-and-rescue teams; medical personnel, equipment, and supplies; and engineers. He also assumed that the Haitian people and responders would need large supplies of food and water. General Keen intended to send these resources and capabilities to Haiti as quickly as possible.[1] As Figure 3.1 illustrates, some of them arrived even before Operation Unified Response and JTF-Haiti were officially established.

The first units assigned to JTF-Haiti were those that DoD had already activated before SOUTHCOM established Operation Unified Response. Among these were several U.S. Navy vessels, including the aircraft carrier USS *Carl Vinson*, and the Global Response Force (GRF), which, at that time, was the 2nd Brigade Combat Team (2 BCT) of 82 AD.[2] Even as many units received WARNORD to prepare for deployment to Haiti on the evening of January 13, the AFSOC 1 SOW had already arrived and reopened Haiti's international airport for flight operations, and USCG vessels had begun delivering emergency supplies and evacuating U.S. citizens (SOUTHCOM, 2010). Other forces flowed in during the next several days. Figure 3.2 shows what units arrived and what other events occurred between January 16 and January 21.

A comparison of Figure 3.1 and Figure 3.2 would suggest that the pace of events began to decrease once the first three days after the earthquake had passed. However, the flow of forces actually increased between January 16 and January 21 as such units as the 22 MEF and more U.S. Navy ships began to arrive, while personnel from the U.S. Army's 82 AD continued to flow in. Also notable in the January 16–21 time frame, as these units began arriving, is that some of them deployed their own field assessment surveillance teams (FASTs) to better determine the requirements they were facing so they could tailor their capabilities more efficiently.

Command and Control of Joint Task Force–Haiti

JTF-Haiti remained under operational control of the SOUTHCOM commander throughout Operation Unified Response. JTF-Haiti held administrative authority and tactical control of multiple subordinate

---

[1] Keen discussion; situation and after-action reports.

[2] The GRF is a designated U.S. Army unit put on round-the-clock alert for immediate deployment to conduct combat operations anywhere in the world within 96 hours.

Figure 3.2
Operation Unified Response Timeline, January 16–21, 2010

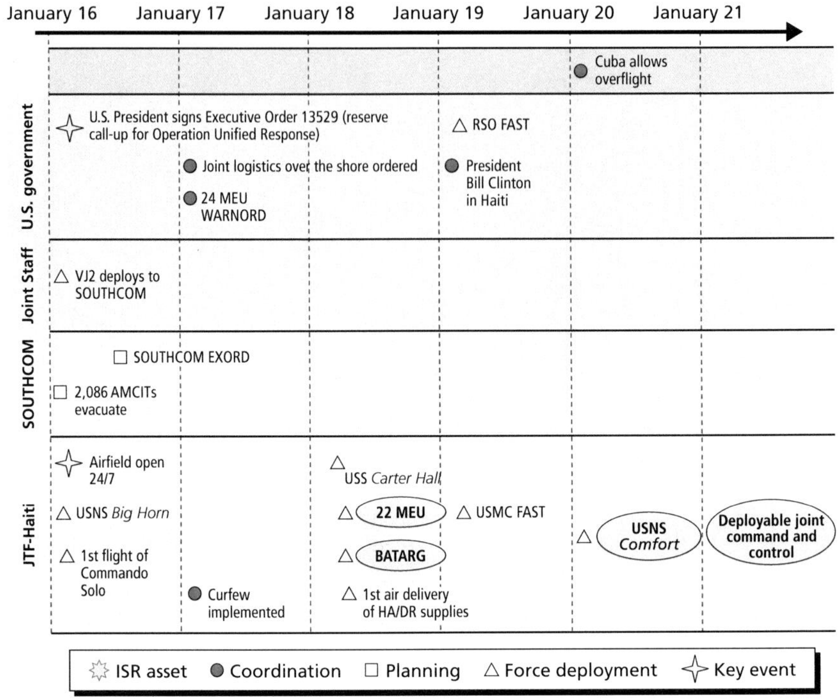

SOURCE: Keen, 2010b.
NOTE: RSO = regional security officer. VJ2 = Vice Director for Intelligence, Joint Staff. USMC = U.S. Marine Corps. BATARG = USS *Bataan* Amphibious Ready Group.
RAND *RR304-3.2*

units made up of active and reserve forces. Figure 3.3 shows the major elements from the Army, Navy, Marine, Air Force, and special operations forces that supported the relief effort as commands subordinate to JTF-Haiti.

As Figure 3.3 indicates, JTF-Haiti stood up two units not seen in previous HA/DR operations: JTF-PO and Joint Logistics Command. Because of the magnitude of the disaster and the critical need to get relief to so many people in need quickly, these commands were formed to expedite reestablishing the country's primary access point, the dock-

Figure 3.3
Joint Task Force–Haiti Organizational Structure

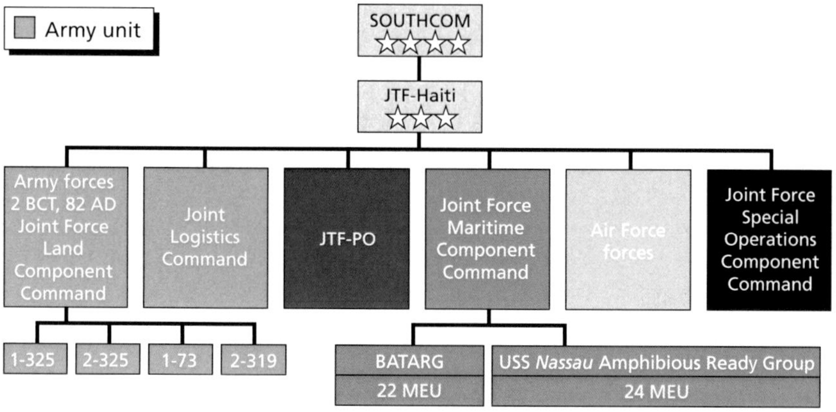

SOURCE: Keen, 2010b.
RAND *RR304-3.3*

ing facilities in Port-au-Prince, and the delivery of emergency materials and supplies (SOUTHCOM, 2010).

The Phases of Operation Unified Response

The original EXORD for the conduct of Operation Unified Response envisioned five distinct phases for the U.S. military HA/DR operations in Haiti:[3]

- *phase I (initial response).* During this phase, the focus is on "immediate lifesaving actions, situational assessment and crisis action planning."
- *phase II (relief).* This phase begins when "forces are deployed or employed to mitigate near-term human suffering in support of USAID/OFDA efforts. Forces will provide immediate disaster relief to assist the affected population. Phase II ends when immediate humanitarian needs have been met (e.g. water, food, shelter,

[3] Different military entities used slightly different phase numbers and descriptions. For example, ARSOUTH phases were phase 1 (initial response), phase 2 (mission preparation), phase 3 (mission execution), and phase 4 (redeployment/restoration).

sanitation, medicine, etc.) and main effort shifts to restoration of key infrastructure."

- *phase III (restoration).* "Phase III begins when immediate humanitarian needs have been met and the main effort shifts to reconstruction of key infrastructure (e.g. roads, power, communications, etc.). Phase III ends when the infrastructure in affected areas is initially rehabilitated to a state where governmental agencies and NGOs can assume their roles in relief and long-term recovery."[4]
- *phase IV (stabilization).* "This phase is required when there is no functioning, legitimate civil governing entity present. The joint force may be required to support other U.S. Government or United Nations (UN) agencies providing limited local governance, integrating the efforts of other supporting/contributing multinational interagency or NGO participants, until legitimate local entities are functioning. This includes providing or assisting in the provision of basic services to the population. Stability operations are necessary to ensure that the effects of the situation leading to the original crisis are mitigated."
- *phase V (recovery).* "This phase is predominantly characterized by support to legitimate civil governance in order to enable civil authority. Phase V begins when the infrastructure in affected areas is initially rehabilitated to a state where governmental agencies and NGOs can assume their roles in relief and long-term recovery. Phase V ends when civil authorities have the capability and capacity to effectively provide HA/DR to their population without U.S. military assistance, regional partnerships and cooperation are enhanced and U.S. military forces safely redeploy."[5]

---

[4] The original order also provided the following: "If a functioning, legitimate civil governing entity exists, Phase III transitions directly to Phase V (Recovery)."

[5] The order further provided the following:

> [Foreign HA]/DR operations always end with Phase V, even when other phases are omitted. (Note: USAID/OFDA, NGOs, [international organizations,] and potentially Army Corps of Engineers will still be providing assistance to civil authorities after Phase V is complete).

The following sections describe how Operation Unified Response activities progressed in accordance with the original intent for Operation Unified Response phases.

Operation Unified Response Phase I: Initial Response

In phase I of Operation Unified Response, JTF-Haiti focused on saving as many lives from immediate peril as possible. JTF-Haiti also began posturing capabilities to support long-term recovery efforts during this period. Activities during the initial response phase included

- evacuating U.S. citizens
- rescuing survivors
- treating and evacuating the injured
- delivering water, food, shelter, and supplies
- restoring essential services and facilities
- supporting long-term recovery efforts.[6]

During this period, JTF-Haiti units and leaders also integrated and coordinated response activities with MINUSTAH security forces, as well as with the many NGOs already in Haiti or arriving shortly after the disaster. JTF-Haiti's relationship with other responders is reviewed in a later section of this chapter.

JTF-Haiti initially established operational headquarters on the U.S. embassy compound in Port-au-Prince. Fortunately, the embassy's buildings were still standing after the earthquake and had functioning communications and essential utilities. Colocating with the embassy staff was also beneficial for the U.S. military to build relationships with the country team and other organizations in the early days of the response. As the operation matured, JTF-Haiti established an independent headquarters and a greater presence within UN clusters and sent

---

[6] This list of activities was drawn from situation reports that JTF-Haiti submitted to SOUTHCOM daily. We reviewed reports dating from January 16 to March 15, 2010.

liaison officers (LNOs) to the MINUSTAH headquarters and other countries that responded (U.S. Joint Forces Command, 2010).[7]

At the peak of the military response on January 31, 2010, JTF-Haiti included more than 22,200 personnel conducting assistance and relief activities across Haiti, working aboard 33 U.S. Navy and USCG vessels and operating more than 300 fixed and rotary-wing aircraft (Keen, Floriano Piexoto, et al., 2010). Figure 3.4 depicts JTF-Haiti's personnel strength over the course of Operation Unified Response.

As Figure 3.4 indicates, significant numbers of U.S. military forces were involved during the first three weeks of Operation Unified Response because they were already present in the area or flowed into the Haiti area of operation very quickly. The VOCO process facilitated a rapid "push" of people and capabilities into JTF-Haiti, allowing it to provide critically needed assistance to victims as quickly as possible. However, the VOCO process also resulted in responders arriving without the situational awareness and direction that a more conventional, condition-based planning approach would have provided (USJFCOM, 2010). Moreover, the rapid rush to get people and resources to the scene before any formal requirements assessment may have resulted in inefficiencies—more of some resources than could be effectively used, and less than was needed of others. We examine these concerns in more detail later in this chapter.

---

[7] The cluster system was introduced as part of the United Nations' 2005 reform of the humanitarian system led by the Emergency Relief Coordinator. This approach tries to clarify the division of labor among organizations and better define roles and responsibilities within the key sectors of the response. Response efforts are currently organized around 11 clusters: logistics; nutrition; emergency shelter; camp management and coordination; health; protection; agriculture; emergency telecommunications; early recovery; education; and water, sanitation, and hygiene. UN and NGO specialists in each of these areas meet periodically (typically daily) in clusters to coordinate efforts and exchange support and ideas. In comparison, the interagency response to U.S. domestic disasters is outlined in the National Response Framework (NRF). This approach organizes responses to disasters in the United States around 15 ESFs: transportation; communications; public works and engineering; firefighting; emergency management; mass care, emergency assistance, housing, and human services; logistics management and resource support; public health and medical services; search and rescue; oil and hazardous-material response; agriculture and natural resources; energy; public safety and security; long-term community recovery; and external affairs.

Figure 3.4
Joint Task Force–Haiti Personnel Strength over Time

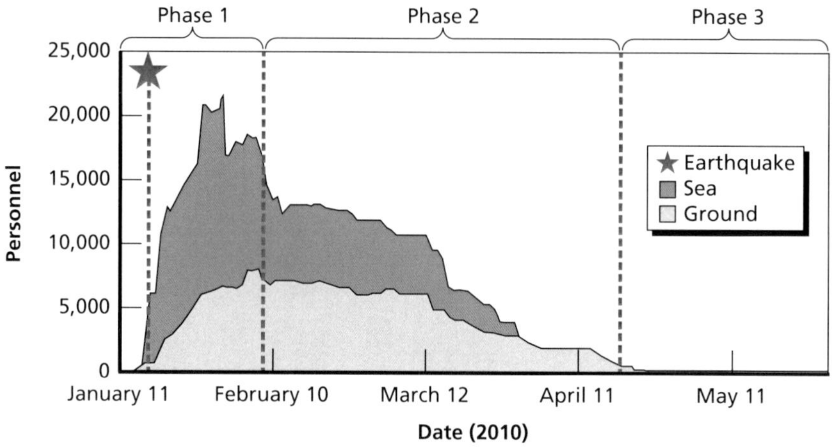

SOURCES: Multiple sources provided by JTF-Haiti and SOUTHCOM.
NOTE: U.S. Marine Corps personnel are included in ground strength.
RAND *RR304-3.4*

Operation Unified Response Phase II: Relief

On February 5, JTF-Haiti transitioned from initial response operations to relief operations. Command priorities shifted from life-saving measures and immediate response efforts to providing assistance and resources for internally displaced persons (IDPs). During the following weeks, JTF-Haiti provided assistance at 16 World Food Programme sites and continued to partner and collaborate with GoH, NGOs, and MINUSTAH forces. JTF relief operations are described in greater detail elsewhere in this chapter.

Operation Unified Response Phase III: Restoration

JTF-Haiti headquarters conducted a relief-in-place from March 15 through March 18, and Operation Unified Response entered a period of support to the restoration of the GoH. The JTF headquarters staff, which was composed primarily of personnel from the XVIII Airborne Corps' ACP, was replaced with staff from the headquarters of ARSOUTH. As part of the transition, General Keen handed over command of JTF-Haiti to MG Simeon Trombitas, formerly the deputy commanding general of JTF-Haiti.

JTF-Haiti's activities during the extended period of restoration-phase operations (mid-March to mid-May) expanded to include planning and coordinating precautions and countermeasures for the floods and mudslides that were likely to occur during the upcoming rainy season (SOUTHCOM, 2010). Heavy rains could have potentially overwhelmed the nine designated IDP camps that JTF-Haiti was assisting in Port-au-Prince and surrounding communities. JTF-Haiti forces helped USAID and MINUSTAH relocate IDPs to newly established transition shelters and camps, and it turned over responsibility for many of the support functions it had been performing to partners in the GoH and MINUSTAH. For example, after a month of shared control of Haiti's international airport, JTF-Haiti's Air Force units turned over complete control of the airfield to the GoH on March 16 (SOUTHCOM, 2010).

Operation Unified Response Phase IV: Stabilization

The stabilization operation planned as phase IV of Operation Unified Response was not carried out. Throughout the relief effort, the citizens of Haiti conducted themselves with admirable order and civility, and MINUSTAH security forces proved capable of handling the few breaches of the peace that did occur. Therefore, SOUTHCOM and JTF-Haiti, in coordination with MINUSTAH and GoH officials, determined that U.S. forces would not need to execute Operation Unified Response phase IV.[8]

Operation Unified Response Phase V: Recovery

During the last days of Operation Unified Response, in late May, JTF-Haiti condensed its force structure in preparation for a full transition of duties to the GoH. Although military forces still contributed to USAID and UN efforts, only a small contingent of U.S. military police and engineers remained with the headquarters on June 1, 2010, when

---

[8] Discussion with General Keen, SOUTHCOM headquarters, Doral, Fla., April 20, 2011, and General Trombitas, ARSOUTH headquarters, San Antonio, Texas, April 8, 2011.

the mission was declared complete. Follow-on missions then fell under a newly formed coordination cell that SOUTHCOM had already been preparing for the New Horizons exercises scheduled to start in July (SOUTHCOM, 2010).

Joint Task Force–Haiti's Relationship with Other Major Actors

Not only was the response to the 2010 Haiti earthquake the largest HA/DR operation ever conducted by the U.S. military, it was the largest international humanitarian response to a natural disaster in history. More than 140 countries and more than 500 NGOs contributed to the Haiti earthquake relief effort (H. Clinton, 2011; Margesson and Taft-Morales, 2010, p. 11). This section describes how JTF-Haiti interacted with the other major actors involved in rendering HA to Haiti.

As James Schear, Deputy Assistant Secretary of Defense for Partnership Strategy and Stability Operations, indicated in his testimony before Congress in July 2010, "one of the great characteristics of the U.S. Government response to Haiti was partnership" (Schear, 2010). The massive relief effort required JTF-Haiti to coordinate with many organizations, including U.S. interagency partners (such as USAID, the U.S. lead federal agency), the GoH, intergovernmental partners (such as foreign militaries and foreign development agencies), multinational partners (including the United Nations Office for the Coordination of Humanitarian Affairs [OCHA] and MINUSTAH), and NGOs from around the world. The challenge was how best to coordinate the efforts of these various actors.

As indicated by the JTF-Haiti commander and the MINUSTAH commander, Major General Floriano Peixoto Vieira Neto, the United States decided early on in the operation not to create a combined (i.e., international) JTF:

> With the UN already on the ground [in Haiti], a robust multinational force was in place. In addition, MINUSTAH countries contributing additional resources and personnel already had links

> to their local UN representatives. Creating a *combined* Joint task force would have conflicted with those efforts. (Keen, Floriano Peixoto, et al., 2010, p. 8)

As a result, JTF-Haiti needed a mechanism through which it could coordinate its efforts with the efforts of its interagency, intergovernmental, multinational, and NGO partners. The coordination mechanism that was established early was JTF-Haiti's HACC.

Joint Task Force–Haiti's Humanitarian Assistance Coordination Center

The HACC served to (1) coordinate, synchronize, track and assess HA operations; (2) create and maintain a humanitarian common operational picture; (3) integrate with all stakeholders in order to develop prioritized lists of support requirements; and (4) serve as the primary JTF interface with UN, NGO, and interagency partners (Operation Unified Response, undated). About half of the HACC's members operated from the U.S. embassy in Port-au-Prince, acting as DoD's interface with OFDA. The HACC's other members worked at the UN Logistics Base, partnering with OCHA, MINUSTAH, partner-nation militaries, and the international humanitarian community within the UN cluster system, which includes civil-military teams focused on such issues as health, food, water, electricity, agriculture, and shelter (Pueschel, 2010). Figure 3.5 illustrates how the HACC was integrated with the major players in the Haiti relief effort, including U.S. interagency partners, JTF-Haiti, and MINUSTAH's Joint Operations and Tasking Centre (JOTC), which served as a focal point for requests from humanitarian organizations for UN and non-UN military, police, and mission logistics assistance (MINUSTAH, undated [b]).

Figure 3.6 illustrates how requests for assistance (RFAs) were formally processed and the role that JTF-Haiti played in that process. As a need arose to support an NGO in providing HA, it was validated in a UN cluster meeting and sent to the MINUSTAH JOTC. If MINUSTAH was unable to provide the assistance requested, U.S. military or other organizations could volunteer to accept the request. USAID then would then the request into a spreadsheet called a Mission

Figure 3.5
Joint Task Force–Haiti Humanitarian Assistance Coordination Center Integration

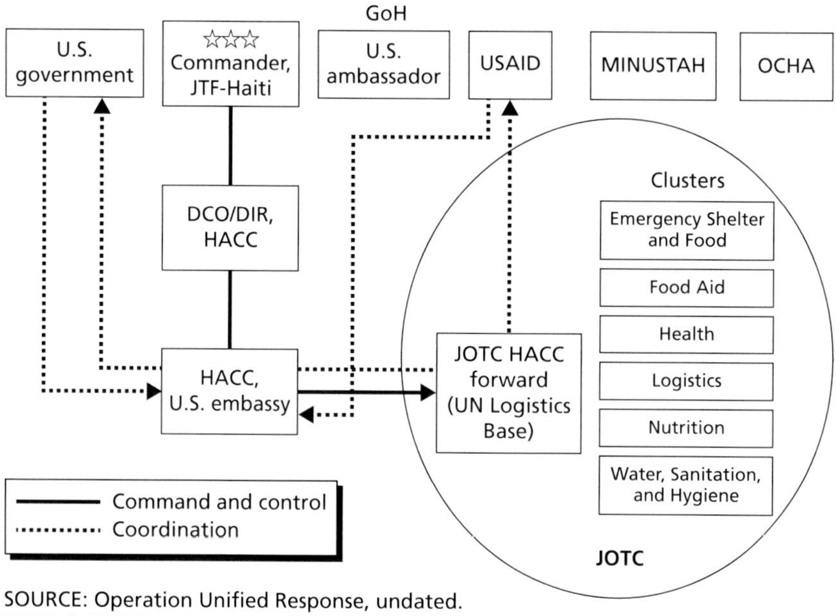

SOURCE: Operation Unified Response, undated.
NOTE: DCO/DIR = deputy commander, operations; director.
RAND *RR304-3.5*

Tasking Matrix (MITAM). JTF-Haiti then processed the MITAM and produced a fragmentary order, which tasked an organization to provide the support requested (Operation Unified Response, undated).

Initially, RFAs were received at the HACC in the U.S. embassy, but, because it was difficult for representatives from NGOs and the United Nations to gain access to the embassy, RFAs were later routed through the UN's JOTC.

A key decision was made by SOUTHCOM and JTF-Haiti to use unclassified information whenever possible and to use public platforms for sharing information in order to facilitate the exchange of information across partners (Keen, Floriano Peixoto, et al., 2010, p. 91). In previous response efforts, much of DoD's information about assistance requests and responses were processed on classified information systems that were inaccessible to the public. During the Haiti response,

Figure 3.6
The Formal Request-for-Assistance Process

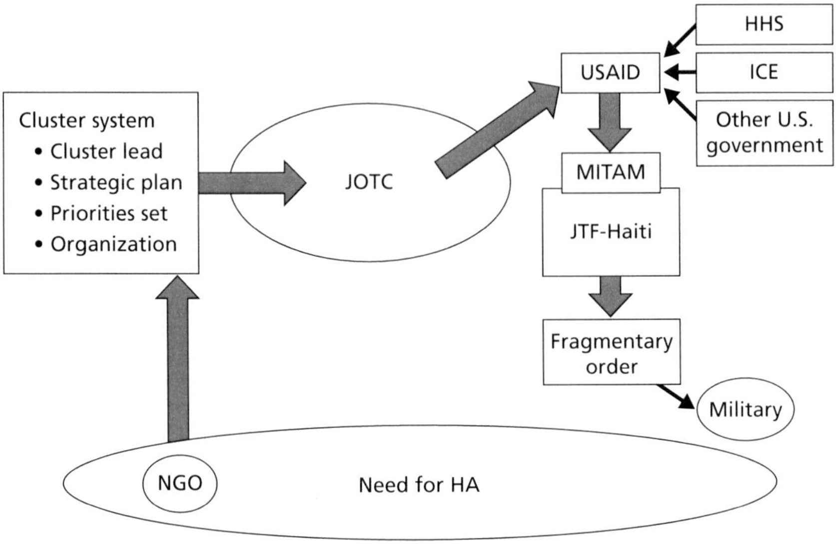

SOURCE: Operation Unified Response, undated.
RAND *RR304-3.6*

nearly all of this information was kept unclassified and shared widely with partners across the Haiti response. SOUTHCOM established the All Partners Access Network (APAN) (originally developed by USPACOM and formerly known as the Asia-Pacific Area Network) as the primary, unclassified, nonmilitary information sharing, collaboration, and communication hub during the Haiti response (Telligent, 2010). SOUTHCOM made password registration available to anyone on request, and, within three weeks, APAN had more than 1,800 registered users (King, 2010). Imagery products, maps, photos, assessments, situation reports, common operational picture reports, and requests for information were all made available on APAN (King, 2010). From the information-management standpoint, the decision to keep the Haiti operations within the unclassified domain enabled a high degree of information sharing across agencies (Schear, 2010).

The HACC played a significant role in the coordination of information and relief efforts across interagency, intergovernmental, multinational, and nongovernmental partners. After the conclusion of Operation Unified Response, General Keen indicated that the success of the operation could not have been achieved "without the strong partnerships that were shared and developed with the GoH, UN, United States Agency for International Development and nongovernmental organization counterparts" (Keen, Floriano Peixoto, et al., 2010, p. 89).

Joint Task Force–Haiti's Relationship with U.S. Interagency Partners

A wide assortment of U.S. government agencies were involved in the response to the Haiti earthquake (see Chapter Two). SOUTHCOM was one of the key agencies involved in the earthquake response. In 2008, in response to a changing regional security environment that included narcotrafficking and other forms of organized crime, SOUTHCOM changed its organizational structure to an enterprise-based model in order to "facilitate collaboration with interagency and other stakeholders, which included a civilian deputy to the commander, interagency representatives embedded in key leadership positions, and a directorate focused on sustaining partnerships" (Pendleton, 2010, p. 20). Figure 3.7 illustrates the organizational structure that SOUTHCOM adopted.

However, a GAO report found that

> SOUTHCOM's support to the disaster relief efforts in Haiti revealed weaknesses in this structure that initially hindered its efforts to conduct a large scale military operation. Specifically, the structure lacked a division to address planning for operations occurring over 30 days to 1 year in duration. In addition, the command's logistics function was suboptimized and had difficulty providing supply and engineering support to the relief effort. (Pendleton, 2010, p. 20)

Discussions we held with U.S. military officials reinforced these findings.

As a result of these challenges, SOUTHCOM's commander made a decision within the first week of the Haiti disaster to return the command to a traditional joint staff organizational structure while retaining elements from the 2008 reorganization. This change reestab-

Figure 3.7
U.S. Southern Command's Organizational Structure After the 2008 Transformation

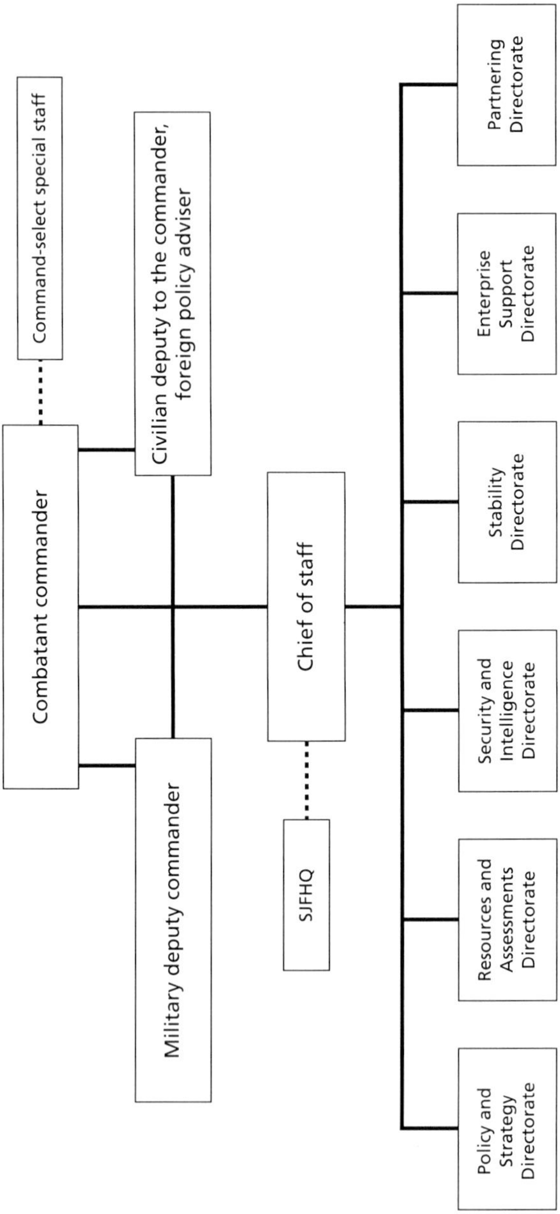

SOURCE: Pendleton, 2010.

RAND *RR304-3.7*

lished the logistics and planning directorates on the SOUTHCOM staff, centralizing those functions and making support from them more readily accessible to counterparts in JTF-Haiti and other military organizations involved in the response effort. Figure 3.8 illustrates the organizational structure that SOUTHCOM adopted during the Haiti earthquake relief efforts.

After this change was made, interagency coordination was much improved. In the following section, we discuss JTF-Haiti's relationship to the Department of State and USAID, the two partners with which it interacted the most. More information about the whole-of-government U.S. response is in Chapter Two.

U.S. Department of State

One of the reasons that the United States was able to respond so quickly to the earthquake was that many of the main players involved already had working relationships with one another because the United States has been involved in Haiti for decades. For instance, when the earthquake struck, Secretary Clinton appointed Cheryl Mills, her chief of staff, to lead the response (rather than the Bureau of Western Hemisphere Affairs) for the Department of State. Mills had already been working on development issues in Haiti and was familiar with the Haitian government and key institutions of the country. In Haiti, the Ambassador Merten led the State Department's efforts. General Keen coordinated directly with the ambassador.

U.S. Agency for International Development

In the immediate aftermath of the earthquake in Haiti, President Obama designated Rajiv Shah, the USAID administrator, as the unified disaster coordinator for the Haiti response. As the lead federal agency in the response, USAID coordinated the efforts of the Department of State, DoD, DHS, and HHS. USAID also worked with the GoH, other foreign governments, the United Nations, other international organizations, and NGOs.

Therefore, DoD was in a supporting role to USAID. However, in some respects, USAID did not have the capacity to lead such a large interagency effort. According to Susan Reichle, USAID deputy assis-

Figure 3.8
U.S. Southern Command's Organizational Structure Adopted During Operation Unified Response

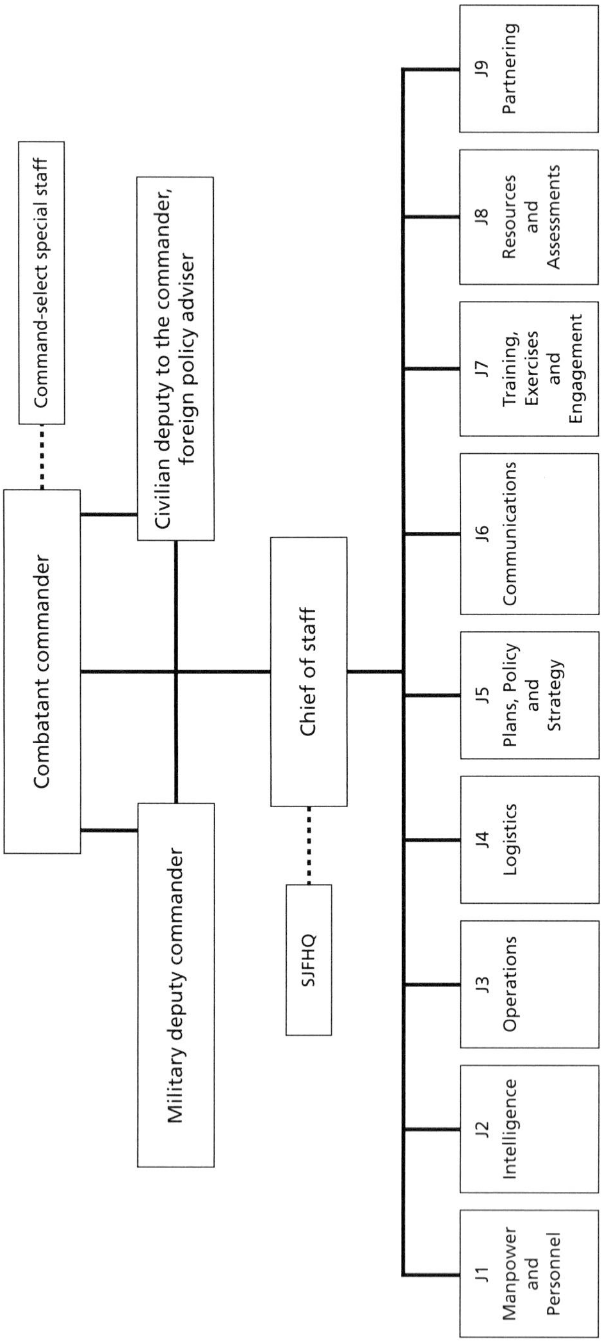

SOURCE: Pendleton, 2010.
RAND *RR304-3.8*

tant administrator, the agency was overwhelmed (Baron, 2010). She said that USAID workers were asking themselves, "How do we lead with such a small agency? We are smaller than the military band" (Baron, 2010).

Typically, in a foreign DR, USAID's OFDA is the lead agency. However, several factors made it particularly difficult for USAID and OFDA to respond to the Haiti earthquake. Most importantly, when the earthquake struck, several key leadership positions at USAID, and especially OFDA, were either vacant or newly appointed. For instance, the USAID administrator had been sworn into office five days before the earthquake hit. In addition, there were vacancies in the following key positions: deputy administrator for USAID, assistant administrator for DCHA, and assistant administrator for OFDA. In Haiti, the new USAID mission director had arrived only 24 hours before the earthquake hit (USAID, 2010a). As a result, because of the scale of the response, USAID deployed additional support through the U.S. Special Coordinator for Relief and Reconstruction.

Recognizing the magnitude of the disaster, and despite the challenges outlined above, USAID deployed a DART to Haiti within hours of the earthquake and took on the role of lead federal agency. General Keen, the JTF-Haiti commander, coordinated directly with USAID. Because SOUTHCOM responds to more humanitarian disasters than other COCOMs do, it has developed a very close working relationship with USAID and the OFDA DART, as well as other interagency partners. For instance, a USAID LNO and an OFDA DART LNO are colocated in SOUTHCOM headquarters.

The Government of Haiti

Within hours of the earthquake, President René Préval sent a representative by motorbike to Ambassador Merten's residence to request immediate assistance from the United States. Given that General Keen was at Ambassador Merten's residence at the time, he was able to relay the Haitian minister's requests to SOUTHCOM as the ambassador was relaying them to other U.S. officials. The first thing the GoH asked DoD to do was open and take control of the Toussaint Louverture International Airport because its terminal had been significantly damaged and its control tower was disabled. On January 13, General Keen met with Haitian government officials and UN officials at the airport, and together they inspected the runway (Keen, Elledge, et al., 2010, p. 85). As the U.S. relief effort matured, the State Department served as the primary liaison to the Haitian government for the U.S. relief effort, and the JTF-Haiti commander coordinated with Haitian government leaders through the U.S. Department of State.

The UN Office for the Coordination of Humanitarian Affairs

The United Nations has been operating in Haiti since 1990 and was closely involved in the 2010 relief effort. OCHA is the primary UN office responsible for coordinating international humanitarian efforts. Figure 3.9 illustrates the international architecture for coordination of HA.

A 2011 evaluation of OCHA's response to the Haiti earthquake found that, "despite the fact that the UN system including UNOCHA was very badly affected by the emergency, they were operational and contributed to the humanitarian response quickly" (Bhattacharjee and Lossio, 2011, p. 9).

Following the earthquake, a UN Humanitarian Civil-Military Coordination (UN-CMCoord) officer was dispatched to SOUTHCOM to facilitate coordination between civilian and military humanitarian efforts (Butterfield, Reario, and Dolan, 2010). In addition, a second UN-CMCoord officer was stationed in Washington to work with the U.S. military and USAID, including OFDA (Butterfield, Reario, and Dolan, 2010). These officers facilitated the exchange of information between UN and U.S. agencies and helped those organizations get access to key decisionmakers on the ground when needed. One of the primary reasons that the UN-CMCoord structure worked well was that key liaison staff from many military and humanitarian organizations were graduates of UN-CMCoord courses run by UN-CMCoord, based in Geneva; therefore, they already knew each other and shared a common professional understanding (Butterfield, Reario, and Dolan, 2010).

Figure 3.9
Architecture for International Humanitarian Coordination

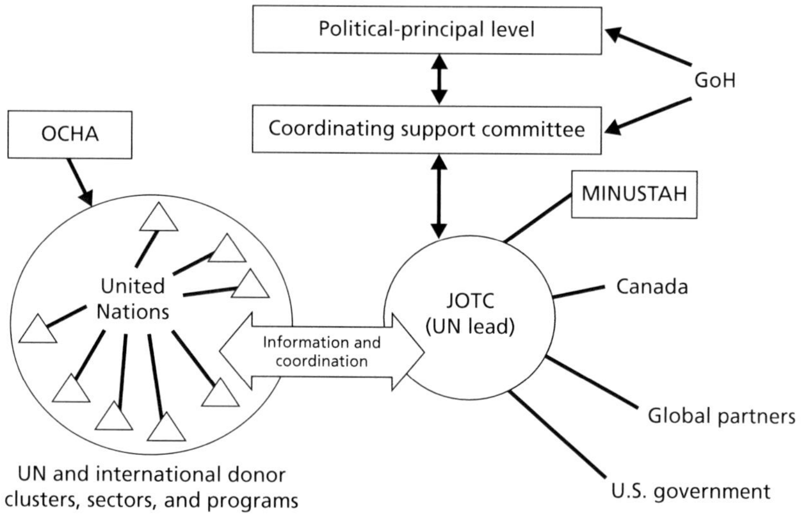

SOURCE: JTF-Haiti.
RAND *RR304-3.9*

The UN Stabilization Mission in Haiti

In April 2004, after the fall of President Jean-Bertrand Aristide, the UN Security Council established MINUSTAH to accomplish the following objectives (MINUSTAH, undated [d]):

- Support the transitional government in ensuring a secure and stable environment.
- Assist in monitoring, restructuring, and reforming the Haitian National Police.
- Help with comprehensive and sustainable disarmament, demobilization, and reintegration programs.
- Assist with the restoration and maintenance of the rule of law, public safety, and public order in Haiti.
- Protect UN personnel, facilities, installations, and equipment, and protect civilians under imminent threat of physical violence.

- Support the constitutional and political processes; assist in organizing, monitoring, and carrying out free and fair municipal, parliamentary, and presidential elections.
- Support the transitional government, as well as Haitian human-rights institutions and groups, in their efforts to promote and protect human rights.
- Monitor and report on the human-rights situation in the country.

MINUSTAH was originally authorized to include up to 6,700 military personnel, 1,622 police, about 550 international civilian personnel, 150 UN volunteers, and about 1,000 local civilian staff (MINUSTAH, undated [c]).

The MINUSTAH headquarters collapsed during the 2010 earthquake, killing 101 UN workers. This loss of UN staff, including the head of mission and his principal deputy, was by far the greatest for any single event in UN peacekeeping's 62-year history (MINUSTAH, undated [a]). This large-scale loss of life severely affected MINUSTAH's capacity to respond to the earthquake. On January 19, 2010, the Security Council endorsed the Secretary-General's recommendation to "increase the overall force levels of MINUSTAH by 2,000 troops and 1,500 police to support immediate recovery, reconstruction, and stability efforts in the country" (MINUSTAH, undated [c]).

On January 26, 2010, MINUSTAH, in coordination with OCHA, established the JOTC (MINUSTAH, 2010). The JOTC served as a single point of contact for requests for military or police assistance. It also eliminated the need for NGOs to have direct contact with the military or police during the request process and allowed for better situational awareness regarding the security needs of NGOs (MINUSTAH, 2010).

A positive, cooperative relationship between MINUSTAH and JTF-Haiti was facilitated by the long-standing friendship between the MINUSTAH military commander, General Floriano Peixoto of Brazil, and General Keen. These officers met in 1984 when they were captains in their respective countries' armies, and they continued their friendship from that time onward (Keen, Floriano Peixoto, et al., 2010,

p. 4). Twenty-six years later, they found themselves working together as general officers coordinating relief efforts in Haiti.

Both leaders thought it imperative to clearly identify the role of each partner to avoid confusion and duplicated effort (Keen, Floriano Peixoto, et al., 2010, p. 8). Because MINUSTAH had been conducting security and stability operations in Haiti since long before the earthquake, Generals Keen and Floriano Peixoto, in consultation with the GoH, SOUTHCOM, and UN officials, agreed that MINUSTAH would continue in that role, allowing JTF-Haiti to focus on providing HA/DR. MINUSTAH would be primarily responsible for security; on any given day, MINUSTAH conducted, on average, more than 600 security operations involving more than 4,500 troops. MINUSTAH proved capable of performing this mission (Keen, Floriano Peixoto, et al., 2010, p. 10). The only security operations that were carried out by JTF-Haiti were in direct support of HA missions. General Floriano Peixoto commented that clearly defining and understanding the role that each partner had in the relief effort was key to their mutual success (Keen, Floriano Peixoto, et al., 2010, p. 10).

Generals Floriano Peixoto and Keen also improved communications and transparency by establishing LNOs in each headquarters; exchanging phone numbers and email addresses of all their branch and section chiefs, senior aides, and advisers; and conducting staff briefings for each other during the first week on the ground (Keen, Floriano Peixoto, et al., 2010, p. 8). General Keen has commented that the combined military presence on the streets of Port-au-Prince made a difference:

> Seeing U.S. Army Soldiers standing side-by-side with MINUSTAH Soldiers at food distribution points during the first few weeks sent a strong message to the Haitian people: partnership and unity of effort. It paved the way for all we would do. (Keen, Floriano Peixoto, et al., 2010, p. 11)

Schear reinforced this notion when he testified to Congress, stating the following:

> The mutually reinforcing relationship between USSOUTHCOM and MINUSTAH enabled the Joint Task Force (JTF) to support the delivery of food, water, and emergency medical care, with MINUSTAH ensuring the necessary security for these activities. (Schear, 2010)

Foreign Militaries

Twenty-six countries provided significant military assets in support of the earthquake response, including field hospitals, troops, military aircraft, hospital ships, cargo ships, port handling equipment, and helicopters (Inter-Agency Standing Committee, 2010, p. 10). Canada, the United States, and the Dominican Republic provided the largest contingents initially (Inter-Agency Standing Committee, 2010, p. 10).

JTF-Haiti received LNOs from Canada, France, and South Korea and had less formal relationships with non-MINUSTAH countries, such as Spain, Italy, Colombia, and Mexico. In addition to these relationships, the U.S. military had additional visibility into the humanitarian operations of foreign militaries through the MINUSTAH JOTC. The UN-CMCoord officer, who was collocated at SOUTHCOM, was also able to provide insight into the coordination of humanitarian operations.

Importantly, Canadian Brigadier General Nicolas Matern was serving as an exchange officer and deputy commanding general of the XVIII Airborne Corps when the earthquake occurred.[9] When that unit's ACP was called upon to serve as the core of JTF-Haiti's headquarters, General Matern deployed with it. Once in country, he was appointed coordinator of HA for JTF-Haiti and its direct liaison to the Canadian military. Canadian Forces deployed approximately 2,000 military personnel to Haiti and provided early assistance with air, land, and maritime components in the cities of Léogâne and Jacmel (Government of Canada, 2011).

---

[9] The Canadian military has been increasingly integrated into U.S. command structures.

Nongovernmental Organizations

Lastly, JTF-Haiti played a vital role in supporting NGOs in distributing aid. According to General Keen,

> There were reportedly over 1,000 NGOs working with the UN Office of Coordination of Humanitarian Assistance (OCHA). NGOs are the scouts and soldiers of the humanitarian effort. They manage IDP camps, food and shelter distributions, establish medicals [sic] facilities, and deliver all types of relief. (Baron, 2010)

The general sense among U.S. government officials with whom we spoke is that the relationship between JTF-Haiti and the NGO community worked quite well. For instance, without the participation of the NGO community, personnel from the USNS *Comfort* would not have been able to successfully perform 843 complex surgeries. Because of ongoing contingencies in the U.S. Central Command (CENTCOM) area of responsibility (AOR), it was extremely difficult for DoD to staff the *Comfort* with the number of surgical specialists required to meet mission requirements. Because of this gap, augmentation with NGO surgical specialists was determined to be appropriate (James and Cubano, 2012). Typically, there are some NGOs that do not want to be publicly associated with the U.S. military, but, for the most part, there was a shared common interest in helping the Haitian people. However, JTF-Haiti did receive some reports that the MITAM process was not responsive enough, and there are several anecdotes of NGOs bypassing the MITAM process to get assistance. The JOTC addressed these problems by serving as the single point of contact for NGO requests for military or police assistance.

Early on in the aftermath of the quake, NGOs were concerned about their safety as they began providing HA. This was especially the case when about 3,000 inmates broke free from the collapsed Haitian National Penitentiary (Cockcroft, 2010). In the end, criminal and gang activity did not have a significant impact on HA efforts. Perhaps this was a result of the large presence of military troops from around the world.

Observations on the U.S. Military Response to the Haiti Earthquake

JTF-Haiti delivered an impressive amount of HA/DR to victims of the Haiti earthquake, and it did so in a timely manner. Doubtless, many people who were in Haiti when the earthquake occurred and are alive today would have perished in the aftermath of this disaster had it not been for the rapid response of the U.S. military. Yet every major military operation faces challenges, and much can be learned by examining how those challenges were met. This section offers observations regarding the U.S. military's performance in Haiti.

Joint Task Force–Haiti's Accomplishments: Performance Versus Effectiveness

JTF-Haiti provided extensive resources, services, and support to the people of Haiti during five months of HA/DR operations. In keeping with the operational tasks previously identified, the following points highlight but a few of the key contributions that JTF-Haiti made during the response and recovery time periods (U.S. Joint Forces Command, 2010):

- evacuated 16,412 U.S. citizens; medically evacuated 343 patients
- delivered more than 2.6 million liters of water, 17 million lb. of bulk food, and 5.7 million individual meals or rations
- conducted more than 1,000 surgeries; treated more than 9,000 patients
- provided emergency shelter for 1.7 million people
- cleared 12,274 cubic yards of rubble and assessed the structural integrity of more than 25,000 buildings and homes
- reopened the airport to operations on January 13, enabling the delivery of 36 tons of emergency relief supplies and equipment
- assisted in reopening docking facilities on January 20, enabling the delivery of more than 8,000 shipping containers.

The foregoing list of achievements is admirable. However, it is notable that every item on the list is a measure of *performance*, not necessarily a measure of *effectiveness*. For instance, JTF-Haiti personnel conducted more than 1,000 surgeries, but what was the total number of injured patients who needed surgery due to injuries sustained in the earthquake? Similarly, JTF-Haiti provided emergency shelter for 1.7 million people, but was that sufficient? If so, then JTF-Haiti was very effective in providing emergency shelter for victims of the Haiti earthquake, but, if twice that number were made homeless in the disaster, then it was substantially less effective than that number might initially indicate. Such numbers are notoriously difficult to obtain for large disasters, but response requirements, such as for emergency shelter, can be refined through assessment during relief operations.

Measuring effectiveness requires not only performance data but also standards against which to measure that performance. Standards can be established only once mission requirements are determined, and, because no formal assessment of mission requirements was performed before forces were selected and deployed, no standards were developed before data collection began (U.S. Joint Forces Command, 2010). According to an operations research and systems analysis (ORSA) specialist who did assessment for the JTF-Haiti senior staff,

> ORSAs had good information, but it was too little, too late, too ineffective. The primary problem was timing. At the beginning, in the emergency crisis action mode, responsibilities and tasks were not specific to units or individuals. After that, the time for assessments had already passed. Most of the other staff members collected data and continued to provide insight to commanders. But in the absence of information gathering priorities, metrics, and data storage, everyone did their own thing—which was good. But the staff specialties and selected importance were not very relevant for the info and measurements needed to inform decision makers.[10]

---

[10] Discussion with an Operation Unified Response participant, spring 2011. We received similar reports in discussions with Joint Center for Operational Analysis analysts who deployed with JTF-Haiti, and they are reflected in findings of a Joint Center for Operational Analysis report on Operation Unified Response dated May 15, 2010, that is not available to the general public.

This does not mean that JTF-Haiti's leaders did not seek to determine mission requirements and adjust their efforts accordingly. By the sixth day of Operation Unified Response, the ORSAs had developed an assessment framework based on operational objectives and assessment metrics similar to what the XVIII Airborne Corps had used in Iraq. However, given differences between wartime missions and HA/DR operations, they had difficulty getting buy-in from other staff elements, and the kind of information reported was often irrelevant or too granular to inform decisionmaking.[11] Ultimately, as Operation Unified Response progressed, JTF-Haiti members identified and refined their mission requirements by coordinating with other response organizations and determining how to best support them and victims of the earthquake. This was a key role of the civil affairs units that worked with the UN clusters, as previously described (see, for example, JTF-Haiti, 2010). They regularly reported this information sharing, collaboration, and coordination in commanders' meetings and situational reports and via LNOs with MINUSTAH. In fact, the JTF-Haiti commander and his deputy commander synchronized their schedules to ensure that at least one of them was always present with troops providing assistance, and the other at coordination meetings.[12]

This approach was probably effective, but, by establishing mission requirements only after the operation had commenced, JTF-Haiti not only lost the ability to develop objective standards for performance evaluation but had also exposed itself to the risk of mission creep. Even before the earthquake, Haiti was significantly impoverished and reliant on outside assistance for survival. The sudden inflow of HA that JTF-Haiti and other responders provided was met by a ready market, one that would have welcomed it to continue indefinitely for ongoing domestic support. JTF-Haiti's fluid approach to identifying mission requirements could easily have evolved into commitments to provide such support.

---

[11] For instance, the medical staff reported the number of centrifuges operating each day. Discussion with an Operation Unified Response participant, spring 2011.

[12] Keen discussion.

That said, this study found little evidence of mission creep in the reports and lessons-learned studies it examined. General Keen made it clear, from his mission statement onward, that JTF-Haiti's ultimate objective was to facilitate the transition of support back to the GoH, United Nations, and USAID at the earliest feasible date. Although establishing mission requirements over the course of the operation may have been a risky approach, in this case, it appears to have worked. The communication and collaboration conducted by JTF-Haiti following the earthquake appears to have enabled military planners and leaders to strike the right balance of effort in the response, meeting the overall intent of the mission.

Other Observations Regarding the Coordination Effort

Four broad themes stand out in JTF-Haiti's experience in coordinating with U.S. interagency partners, international organizations, foreign militaries, and the NGO community. First, the Haiti experience reinforces the general notion that, during DR, communication can be improved if the different players have existing relationships already in place. Because the international community has been involved in Haiti for the past 30 years, many of those relationships were already established when the earthquake occurred. Many U.S. officials knew key officials in the Haitian government, as well as UN officials working in country. In addition, the long-standing role of the United Nations in Haiti provided a logical conduit for countries to tap into for their own relief efforts. Lastly, the relationship between Generals Floriano Peixoto and Keen demonstrates that personnel exchanges between countries or between agencies can be extremely beneficial in the long term. Such exchanges provide a better understanding of the culture of the other country or organization, and these lasting friendships have the potential to improve future disaster-response efforts. One way to maintain these relationships is to regularly conduct interagency and international emergency-preparedness exercises.

Second, it is important to recognize that JTF-Haiti's success in sharing information with other countries and NGOs was largely due to the fact that it did not classify most of that information. Classifying information would have prevented it from being shared with NGOs.

Our discussions with military officials indicate that those involved in JTF-Haiti feel quite strongly about the need to restrict any classification standards for HA missions.

Third, a common theme in discussions with senior military leaders, as well as with civilian responders, was that the military service members of JTF-Haiti were better prepared for the civil affairs–related demands of this mission than for previous humanitarian relief efforts. The evidence was anecdotal but often repeated that servicemembers' experience in Iraq and Afghanistan prepared them to interact with and assist civilian populations of different languages and cultural backgrounds. Any military response to a disaster is challenged with the need to balance an effective security posture with an open hand of assistance. By many accounts, servicemembers with recent experience in urban combat operations took naturally to striking such a balance, not just with the Haitian population but also with civilian and other military response partners. This experience might benefit future relief operations by codifying the training and experiences of these combat veterans specifically for humanitarian missions.

Fourth, the strengths and weaknesses of the MINUSTAH JOTC should be examined in depth to determine whether this is a model that should be used in future DRs. The JOTC seemed to work well in coordinating across the international humanitarian response architecture, including the U.S. military response. However, the pros and cons of the JOTC model need to be more fully investigated. Haiti was a singular case, not only in the amount of destruction caused by the earthquake but also because the country was already reliant on foreign assistance, with many aid organizations already present. Haiti is also in SOUTHCOM's AOR, and that command includes staff members who were familiar with the Haitian government, culture, and language. Relationships among governments and responding organizations in Haiti were already established in many cases. This will not always be the case before a disaster occurs in another country, and it is not clear how effective the JOTC model would be absent these relationships. The JOTC model should be tested through exercises involving scenarios of varying levels of disaster severity and varying degrees of existing relationship among responding organizations.

CHAPTER FOUR

Findings and Recommendations

By most accounts, the United States' large and rapid response to the Haiti earthquake was both a direct source of needed assistance to the people of Haiti and a major contribution to the multinational relief effort. The U.S. military played a key role in that response, likely saving many lives and easing the suffering of thousands of victims. Nevertheless, our research indicates that improvements could be made that would reduce the number and severity of challenges that future relief efforts might face when responding to foreign disasters, particularly if the United States is committed to whole-of-government responses to future disasters that strike its neighbors and allies. This chapter presents the findings of our research and offers the U.S. government overall, DoD in particular, and most specifically the U.S. Army recommendations for how future similar efforts might be done more efficiently and effectively.

Findings

Ample U.S. Legal Authority Exists for Foreign Humanitarian Assistance and Disaster Relief Operations, but the Key DoD Policy Needs to Be Updated

As we discuss in detail in Chapter Two, there is ample statutory authority in Title 10 of the U.S. Code for components of DoD to provide a wide range of HA/DR. However, the version of DoDD 5100.46, which provides guidance on DoD roles in foreign DR, that was in effect when earthquake relief operations began was dated December 3, 1975.[1] This directive specifies the process by which SecDef responds to requests for DoD participation in foreign HA/DR operations. But it the 1975 version cited none of the specific Title 10 sections authorizing such DoD activities because all were enacted and have been amended subsequent to its publication. It also contained outmoded references to DoD and State Department entities.

By contrast, other similar DoD directives and instructions are significantly more current, including ones dealing with discrete parts of HA/DR, and one for DoD response to international CBRNE incidents. Similarly, related joint doctrine on HA/DR is much more current than DoDD 5100.46. Updating the DoDD will ensure that similar missions in the future have the appropriate, current supporting policies and direction.

Mass and Initiative Enabled a Prompt, Robust Response

JTF-Haiti's delivery of goods and services was very responsive and robust. General Keen's informal approach to determining initial requirements and his use of VOCO for force selection and assignment generated a top-down push that resulted in a high volume of people and resources to the relief effort quickly. Although U.S. military leaders arrived with little situational awareness and direction, they were given significant latitude to exercise initiative in directing the response effort, immediately seeking out victims, joining in rescue operations, distributing supplies, and providing whatever other relief services seemed to be needed. As JTF-Haiti became more organized, its leaders took a more deliberate approach to determining mission requirements. They systematically engaged U.S. non-DoD, GoH, UN, NGO, and foreign military representatives, both directly and in UN cluster meetings, in addition to interacting with earthquake victims, and they used information gathered in these exchanges to adjust mission requirements and focus relief efforts more precisely.

---

[1] This discussion refers to the 1975 DoDD, which was in force during the response to the Haiti earthquake, and it has since been revised.

Planning and Coordination Shortfalls Hindered Efficiency

Although JTF-Haiti led a prompt, robust response, planning and coordination shortfalls hindered its efficiency and, potentially, its effectiveness. The relief effort in Haiti was accomplished without the benefit of well-established plans within SOUTHCOM for such a mission because those plans were still being developed and did not take into account the scale of devastation that Haiti experienced. Moreover, the SOUTHCOM staff was organized to optimize support for operations combating narcotrafficking and other forms of organized crime, versus the kind of large-scale military effort that Operation Unified Response entailed. As a result, the SOUTHCOM staff had difficulty coordinating with the other organizations supporting the effort until it reorganized shortly after Operation Unified Response began.

A more serious problem was that the informal, top-down process that pushed resources to the effort so quickly generated inefficiencies that might have impaired the operation's effectiveness. In estimating initial mission requirements and rushing high volumes of people, equipment, and supplies forward, the operation was likely flooded with more of some resources than were needed and less than were needed of others. This may have hindered performance and effectiveness in key areas; however, it is difficult to tell whether that occurred, and it is even more difficult to suggest a more systematic method of efficiency without a large-scale effort to plan such operations in detail for the future. The lack of formal, condition-based planning at the outset of Operation Unified Response made it impossible to establish metrics with which to measure JTF-Haiti's performance. Such metrics could have been developed over the course of the operation, as information was gathered and requirements refined, but discussions with participants indicate that these measures were not taken. As a result, JTF-Haiti leaders collected a great deal of performance data, but they measured little that would demonstrate Operation Unified Response's effectiveness.

Joint Task Force–Haiti Owed Much of Its Success to Serendipity

Although the lack of metrics makes it impossible to measure JTF-Haiti's effectiveness, the sheer volume of aid reported in the performance data does suggest that Operation Unified Response provided critically needed assistance to many thousands of earthquake victims. Moreover, anecdotal stories of participants and published accounts of MINUSTAH leaders indicate that JTF-Haiti was a critical enabler of their efforts and a positive force in the broader multinational response. This suggests that JTF-Haiti's efforts were largely *successful*, even if *unmeasurable* in a statistically meaningful way.

The approach that General Keen and SOUTHCOM used to rush resources to the operation might be one of the reasons for its success. The use of VOCOs and General Keen's initiative to request and deploy a headquarters and forces as quickly as possible were impressive. If this approach is considered the most effective for similar missions in the future, DoD leaders should consider institutionalizing this process. Before drawing this conclusion, however, consider that other factors have contributed to Operation Unified Response's success. Operation Unified Response was defined by conditions that worked serendipitously to the advantage of JTF-Haiti. JTF-Haiti benefited greatly from the following chance circumstances:

- SOUTHCOM deputy commander General Keen was in Haiti and at U.S. Ambassador Merten's residence when the earthquake struck, placing him in an optimal position to coordinate the military portion of the whole-of-government response.
- Ambassador Merten's residence withstood the earthquake, and the communication equipment there remained functional, which was key to the coordination of JTF-Haiti and the early deployment of military forces.
- General Keen was a longtime colleague of MINUSTAH commander General Floriano Peixoto; their relationship was a foundation for early and continual coordination between MINUSTAH and JTF-Haiti.
- The GRF was available for rapid deployment to JTF-Haiti, but this might not always be the case.
- The JTF-Haiti commander, General Keen, used his professional relationship with the XVIII Airborne Corps commander to deploy a much-needed headquarters element to lead the JTF.

- Many soldiers and marines assigned to JTF-Haiti had a high level of experience in civil affairs and other aspects of working with local citizens, having served repeated tours of duty in Iraq and Afghanistan.

Recommendations

Although some of the recommendations that follow are the responsibility of other government entities instead of or in addition to the Army, we believe nevertheless that—as the major U.S. participant in most efforts of this nature—the Army is in one of the best positions to propose the implementation of measures to improve the timeliness and effectiveness of U.S. foreign HA/DR.

Update the Department of Defense Directive for Foreign Humanitarian Assistance and Disaster Relief

We recommend a comprehensive rewrite and republication of DoDD 5100.46, currently directed at foreign DR. As noted earlier, the directive that was in effect at the time of the earthquake was significantly out of date.[2] Implementation of this recommendation will not only describe the important statutory and other organization structural changes that having taken place but can provide important policy guidance to DoD entities and their government and nongovernment partners on the nature and limitations of the DoD response.

Create a National Framework for Foreign Humanitarian Assistance and Disaster Relief

We recommend the creation of a national framework for foreign HA/DR, similar to the NRF in place for domestic incidents. We learned in our discussions with key leaders in Operation Unified Response

[2] This discussion refers to the 1975 DoDD, which was in force during the response to the Haiti earthquake, and it has since been revised.

that the NRF was actually used to guide certain aspects of the Haiti response.[3]

Nonetheless, the lead-agency responsibilities and many of the relationships required in a foreign response are very different from those in the NRF. Moreover, the NRF—by its own description—is almost exclusively for response operations and does not cover most pre-incident planning and other preparedness functions.

Although DoD and USAID have a standing agreement in place that provides information on the relationship of those two entities for such activities, a national framework for U.S. foreign HA/DR could document and guide a whole-of-government approach for U.S. efforts, not only for U.S. government participants but also for allied governments and NGOs. It could serve as the comprehensive guide for planning, training, and exercises and describe the basic operational structures and processes for a wide range of response activities.

Ensure Familiarity with the Humanitarian Assistance and Disaster Relief Joint Task Force Commander's Handbook

We recommend that the Army ensure that all senior Army commanders are familiar with the guidance provided in *Department of Defense Support to Foreign Disaster Relief (Handbook for JTF Commanders and Below)* (Office of the Deputy Assistant Secretary of Defense for Partnership Strategy and Stability Operations, 2011). No commander's handbook for HA/DR operations existed when the Haiti earthquake occurred. Following that disaster, the U.S. Army began work on a commander's handbook, but it did not reach final publication. In July 2011, DoD published the aforementioned handbook for JTF commanders and subordinate-unit commanders supporting foreign DR operations. This publication lays out U.S. government roles and responsibilities,

---

[3] General Keen indicated that he saw the role of U.S. Ambassador Merten to be, essentially, parallel with that of the principal federal official in a U.S. domestic DR, as specified in the NRF; however, Ambassador Merten lacked the staff typically available to a principal federal official. Therefore, General Keen endeavored to provide him the necessary staff support to perform that function, assuring him, "My staff is your staff." General Keen went on to say that the U.S. NRF has been influential in guiding UN efforts to codify leadership and coordination in international DR efforts.

explains the U.S. foreign DR response process, and provides detailed guidance on how to plan and execute operations in response to a wide range of disasters in cooperation with foreign military and civil authorities and NGOs. The handbook should be required reading at Army intermediate and senior service schools.

Consider a Standing Organization

We recommend further research into the advantages of and justification for establishing a standing organization for HA/DR activities. Such an entity would require personnel and resources, which may be hard to justify in times of fiscal austerity, to prepare for responding to disasters, the frequency of which are impossible to predict. However, a standing organization could perform several important functions—pre-incident, during a response, and post-incident. Those functions could include

- developing doctrine for HA/DR activities
- serving as the focal point for planning, training, and exercises
- establishing metrics and other measures for timely and effective response
- identifying and tracking the preparedness and availability of specialized units and personnel
- providing a base for HA/DR expertise, staff augmentation, equipment, and logistics support
- serving as the central node for interagency, intergovernmental, and nongovernmental collaboration
- conducting initial assessments of requirements for HA/DR operations
- maintaining historical data on HA/DR operations.

A standing organization, if justified, could be established and operated exclusively within DoD, or it might be an interagency entity. Although it is not presently clear what the organizational structure and dedicated resources should be for such an organization, there are several models that could be considered, described in the rest of this section.

Joint Interagency Task Force

The U.S. government has had success in the creation and operation of joint interagency task forces (JIATFs) for other purposes. Notable examples include JIATF South and JIATF West for drug interdiction activities.

JIATF South could be called the "federal-agency" model. It includes representatives from CBP, ICE, and USCG from DHS; the Federal Bureau of Investigation and the Drug Enforcement Administration from Department of Justice; DoD military and civilian representatives (from SOUTHCOM, all services, the Army National Guard, and several DoD intelligence entities); and the Central Intelligence Agency.[4] An entity of this type for foreign HA/DR could bring together key players from numerous, relevant agencies to perform the functions described above across the U.S. government.

JIATF West includes not only most of the member entities in JIATF South but also the Australian Customs Service, the Australian Federal Police, and the New Zealand Police.[5]

Although DoD plays a major role in each of these JIATFs, neither it nor any other agency has traditional command-and-control authority over all member entities. The JIATFs are a collaborative effort, with each agency controlling its own personnel and resources. That would likely be the preferred model for an HA/DR JIATF.

Department of Defense Standing Joint Task Force for Humanitarian Assistance and Disaster Relief

In most cases, the DoD entity for conducting these activities has been ad hoc. In lieu of a standing organization for each geographic COCOM, a centralized standing JTF could serve as the foundation for a DoD response anywhere in the world and could be augmented by expertise and additional resources from the COCOM where the incident is occurring. This structure could be one centralized alternative to the potential elimination of the COCOM SJFHQ. (See Chapter Two for further discussion.)

---

4 For more information, see JIATF South, undated.

5 For more information, see USPACOM, 2013.

Canadian Forces Disaster Assistance Response Team

According to Government of Canada (2005), "[t]he DART is a military organization designed to deploy rapidly anywhere in the world" to provide assistance in the early stages of a disaster. It is made up of approximately 200 Canadian Forces personnel with an ability to operate for up to 40 days. It can be activated at the request of a foreign government or the United Nations, with the collective approval of the Canadian Department of National Defence, Foreign Affairs and International Trade, and the Canadian International Development Agency.

The DART is designed to provide

> primary medical care; production of safe drinking water; a limited specialist engineer capability; and a command and control structure that allows for effective communications between the DART, the host nation, and the other agencies involved in the relief effort, including international organizations, non-governmental organizations and UN aid agencies. (Government of Canada, 2005)

The DART is composed of

- DART headquarters, consisting of about 45 personnel, responsible for command and control in theater and for coordination with the host nation and officials of international organizations and NGOs
- a logistics platoon of "about 20 personnel, responsible for the logistical support services essential to the sustainment of the DART"
- the headquarters of the various DART subunits deployed on the mission, each made up of about nine personnel, to provide the day-to-day command and control of the following DART subunits:
  - an engineer troop of "about 37 personnel, including both field and construction engineers. The field engineer element consists of a water supply section, a field engineer section and a heavy equipment section."
  - a medical platoon of "approximately 40 personnel [that can] provide support to area hospitals or to operate a small medical

aid station, a tented facility capable of providing care for 200 to 250 out-patients and 10 in-patients per day, depending on the requirements of the mission"
– a defense and security platoon of "about 45 personnel to provide . . . security and general support for DART operations."[6]

The Advantages and Disadvantages of Alternative Models

Each of the aforementioned models offers certain advantages and disadvantages in comparison with the others. The JIATF approach would facilitate high-level national and international collaboration; however, it might have difficulty identifying and tracking the preparedness and availability of specialized units and personnel, and it would likely be hampered in efforts to develop doctrine for HA/DR activities because those are essentially military functions. At the other extreme, a DART-like organization could provide a base for HA/DR expertise, staff augmentation, equipment, and logistics support. It also could establish metrics and play a key role in the development of doctrine. But a small organization such as this might have difficulty facilitating interagency, intergovernmental, and international planning and collaboration, particularly if it is situated in a military command and staffed predominantly with military personnel.

A central issue to consider when weighing alternative models is the level in the U.S. command structure at which a standing HA/DR organization should be placed. A national-level organization would be able to standardize procedures and metrics across the various COCOMs, and it would be well placed for collaborating with other DR organizations, nationally and internationally. However, such an organization would be less capable than the COCOMs of understanding the cultural peculiarities of each region or establishing the relationships with principals there that helped make Operation Unified Response effective.

Finally, one must consider the question of whether the standing HA/DR organization should be an interagency, joint, or service entity. Disaster response operations are inherently interagency and joint

---

[6] For more information on the Canadian Forces DART, see Government of Canada, 2005.

endeavors; however, the U.S. Army often provides the lion's share of responders on the ground. It might be best placed to identify and track the preparedness and availability of its specialized units and personnel; take the lead in the development of HA/DR doctrine and metrics; and serve as the focal point for planning, training, and exercises across the U.S. HA/DR community.

Additional study on HA/DR operations across multiple cases should be undertaken before a final decision is made regarding whether a standing organization is warranted and, if so, how and where it should be organized.

Conclusion

Operation Unified Response, the U.S. military's response to the Haiti earthquake, was remarkable in its scope and responsiveness and, by many accounts, saved many lives and alleviated the suffering of many Haitian people. The success of Operation Unified Response, however, was rather serendipitous and due to circumstance and the ingenuity of its leaders. DoD and the services—including the Army in particular, which plays a significant role in these types of operations—should consider carefully both the circumstances surrounding the Haiti earthquake response and the innovative actions of the Operation Unified Response leaders, in order to institutionalize the processes by which Operation Unified Response was successful, in preparation for similar future missions.

References

Baron, Kevin, "After Haiti Earthquake, a Call for More Military Disaster Planning," *Stars and Stripes*, May 31, 2010. As of May 17, 2013:
http://www.stripes.com/news/after-haiti-earthquake-a-call-for-more-military-disaster-planning-1.104954

Bhattacharjee, Abhijit, and Roberta Lossio, *Evaluation of OCHA Response to the Haiti Earthquake*, New York: United Nations Office for the Coordination of Humanitarian Affairs, January 2011. As of May 17, 2013:
https://ochanet.unocha.org/p/Documents/Evaluation%20of%20OCHA%20Response%20to%20the%20Haiti%20Earthquake.pdf

"Bush Aims to Boost US Tsunami Aid," BBC News, February 10, 2005. As of May 20, 2013:
http://news.bbc.co.uk/2/hi/americas/4252171.stm

Butterfield, Alan, Ronaldo Reario, and Robert Dolan, "The United Nations Humanitarian Civil–Military Coordination (UN-CMCoord) Response to the Haiti Earthquake," *Humanitarian Exchange Magazine*, Vol. 48, October 2010. As of May 17, 2013:
http://www.odihpn.org/humanitarian-exchange-magazine/issue-48/the-united-nations-humanitarian-civil%E2%80%93military-coordination-un%E2%80%93cmcoord-response-to-the-haiti-earthquake

Carter, James Earl Jr., *Administration of Foreign Assistance and Related Functions*, Washington, D.C.: White House, Executive Order 12163, September 29, 1979. As of May 20, 2013:
http://www.archives.gov/federal-register/codification/executive-order/12163.html

Cecchine, Gary, Michael A. Wermuth, Roger C. Molander, K. Scott McMahon, Jesse D. Malkin, Jennifer Brower, John D. Woodward, and Donna F. Barbisch, *Triage for Civil Support: Using Military Medical Assets to Respond to Terrorist Attacks*, Santa Monica, Calif.: RAND Corporation, MG-217-OSD, 2004. As of June 14, 2013:
http://www.rand.org/pubs/monographs/MG217.html

Centers for Disease Control and Prevention, "CDC Responds to the Haiti Earthquake," December 29, 2010. As of July 19, 2011:
http://emergency.cdc.gov/disasters/earthquakes/haiti/cdc_earthquake_response.asp

Clinton, Hillary Rodham, "One Year Commemoration of Haiti's Earthquake," Washington, D.C.: U.S. Department of State, press statement, January 11, 2011. As of June 20, 2011:
http://www.state.gov/secretary/rm/2011/01/154303.htm

Clinton, William Jefferson, *Foreign Disaster Assistance*, Washington, D.C.: White House, Executive Order 12966, July 14, 1995. As of May 20, 2013:
http://www.gpo.gov/fdsys/pkg/FR-1995-07-18/pdf/95-17828.pdf

Cockcroft, Lucy, "Haiti Earthquake: Criminal Gangs Return to Rule Slums After Escaping from Prison," *Telegraph*, January 17, 2010. As of May 17, 2013:
http://www.telegraph.co.uk/news/worldnews/centralamericaandthecaribbean/haiti/7010543/
Haiti-earthquake-criminal-gangs-return-to-rule-slums-after-escaping-from-prison.html

Davis, Lynn E., David E. Mosher, Rick Brennan Jr., Michael D. Greenberg, K. Scott McMahon, and Charles W. Yost, *Army Forces for Homeland Security*, Santa Monica, Calif.: RAND Corporation, MG-221-A, 2004. As of June 14, 2013:
http://www.rand.org/pubs/monographs/MG221.html

Davis, Lynn E., Jill Rough, Gary Cecchine, Agnes Gereben Schaefer, and Laurinda L. Rohn, *Hurricane Katrina: Lessons for Army Planning and Operations*, Santa Monica, Calif.: RAND Corporation, MG-603-A, 2007. As of June 14, 2013:
http://www.rand.org/pubs/monographs/MG603.html

Defense Security Cooperation Agency, "Humanitarian Assistance, Disaster Relief and Mine Action (HDM)," last revised April 10, 2013. As of May 20, 2013:
http://www.dsca.osd.mil/programs/HA/HA.htm

DoDD 5100.01—*See* U.S. Department of Defense, 2010.

Doerge, Wally, "Rapid Response: Consular Affairs Task Forces Respond to Quake," *State Magazine*, March 2010, p. 15. As of May 17, 2013:
http://digitaledition.state.gov/publication/?i=85190&p=17

Doscher, Thomas J., "USNORTHCOM Disestablishes SJFHQ," U.S. Northern Command, May 10, 2011. As of August 25, 2011:
http://www.northcom.mil/news/2011/051011.html

DSCA—*See* Defense Security Cooperation Agency.

Duryée, Kathy, *Rapid Assessment Report: Haiti Earthquake Response*, World Vision Haiti, March 2010.

Eberhard, Marc O., Steven Baldridge, Justin Marshall, Walter Mooney, and Glenn J. Rix, *The MW 7.0 Haiti Earthquake of January 12, 2010: USGS/EERI Advance Reconnaissance Team—Team Report V. 1.1*, February 23, 2010. As of July 19, 2011:
http://www.eqclearinghouse.org/20100112-haiti/wp-content/uploads/2010/02/USGS_EERI_HAITI_V1.1.pdf

Federal Emergency Management Agency, *Director Battle Book*, undated.

———, "National Situation Update: Saturday, January 16, 2010," January 20, 2010. As of May 17, 2013:
http://coop.fema.gov/emergency/reports/2010/nat011610.shtm

"First U.S. Vessel Arrives at Port-au-Prince," MSNBC.com news services, January 13, 2010. As of May 17, 2013:
http://www.nbcnews.com/id/34832613/ns/world_news-haiti/t/first-us-vessel-arrives-port-au-prince/#.UZbKiyvF1MY

Fraser, Gen. Douglas M., and Maj. Wendell S. Hertzelle, U.S. Air Force, "Haiti Relief: An International Effort Enabled Through Air, Space, and Cyberspace," *Air and Space Power Journal*, Vol. 5, No. 12, Winter 2010, pp. 5–12. As of May 20, 2013:
http://www.airpower.au.af.mil/airchronicles/apj/apj10/win10/2010_4_03_fraser.pdf

Government of Canada, "Canadian Forces Disaster Assistance Response Team," BG-04.002E, January 10, 2005.

———, "Canada's Response to the Devastating Earthquake," January 11, 2011. As of July 24, 2011:
http://www.canadainternational.gc.ca/haiti/engagement/earthquake-seisme.aspx?view=d

Guha-Sapir, Debarati, Thomas Kirsch, Adam Sirois, and Shayna Dooling, *Report on an Independent Review of the USG Response to the Haiti Earthquake: Findings and Recommendations*, draft, September 28, 2010.

Inter-Agency Standing Committee, *Response to the Humanitarian Crisis in Haiti Following the 12 January 2010 Earthquake: Achievements, Challenges, and Lessons to Be Learned*, July 2010.

James, Terbush, and Miguel Cubano, "DoD and NGOs in Haiti: A Successful Partnership," *World Medical and Health Policy*, Vol. 4, No. 2, July 2012, pp. 1–6.

Jet Propulsion Laboratory, "NASA Airborne Radar Studies Haiti Earthquake Faults," press release, January 26, 2010. As of July 19, 2011:
http://www.jpl.nasa.gov/news/news.cfm?release=2010-031

JIATF South—*See* Joint Interagency Task Force South.

Joint Chiefs of Staff, *Foreign Humanitarian Assistance*, Washington, D.C., Joint Publication 3-29, March 17, 2009. As of May 20, 2013: http://www.dtic.mil/doctrine/new_pubs/jp3_29.pdf

Joint Interagency Task Force South, undated home page. As of May 20, 2013: http://www.jiatfs.southcom.mil/index.aspx

Joint Task Force–Haiti, "Mission Update Brief: Operation Unified Response," briefing slides, January 31, 2010.

JP 3-29—*See* Joint Chiefs of Staff, 2009.

JTF-Haiti—*See* Joint Task Force–Haiti.

Keen, LTG P. K., military deputy commander, U.S. Southern Command, discussion with Gary Cecchine and Forrest E. Morgan, Miami, Fla., April 20, 2010a.

———, "JTF-Haiti Observations and Recommendations," briefing slides provided to the authors, August 25, 2010b.

Keen, LTG P. K., LTC Matthew G. Elledge, LTC Charles W. Nolan, LTC Jennifer L. Kimmey, U.S. Army, "Foreign Disaster Response: Joint Task Force–Haiti Observations," *Military Review*, November–December 2010, pp. 85–96. As of May 17, 2013: http://usacac.army.mil/CAC2/MilitaryReview/Archives/English/MilitaryReview_20101231_art015.pdf

Keen, LTG P. K., U.S. Army, Major General Floriano Peixoto Vieira Neto, Army of Brazil, LTC Charles W. Nolan, U.S. Army, LTC Jennifer L. Kimmey, U.S. Army, and CDR Joseph Althouse, U.S. Coast Guard, "Relationships Matter: Humanitarian Assistance and Disaster Relief in Haiti," *Military Review*, May–June 2010, pp. 2–12. As of May 17, 2013: http://usacac.army.mil/CAC2/MilitaryReview/Archives/English/MilitaryReview_20100630_art004.pdf

Kelley, Joseph E., *Department of Defense: Changes Needed to the Humanitarian and Civic Assistance Program*, Washington, D.C.: U.S. General Accounting Office, GAO/NSIAD-94-57, November 2, 1993. As of May 17, 2013: http://www.gao.gov/products/NSIAD-94-57

King, Dennis, "The Haiti Earthquake: Breaking New Ground in the Humanitarian Information Landscape," *Humanitarian Exchange Magazine*, Vol. 48, October 2010. As of May 17, 2013: http://www.odihpn.org/humanitarian-exchange-magazine/issue-48/the-haiti-earthquake-breaking-new-ground-in-the-humanitarian-information-landscape

Margesson, Rhoda, and Maureen Taft-Morales, *Haiti Earthquake: Crisis and Response*, Washington, D.C.: Congressional Research Service, March 8, 2010.

MINUSTAH—*See* United Nations Stabilization Mission in Haiti.

Obama, Barack, "Organization of the National Security Council System," Washington, D.C., Presidential Policy Directive 1, February 13, 2009. As of May 17, 2013:
https://www.fas.org/irp/offdocs/ppd/ppd-1.pdf

Office of the Deputy Assistant Secretary of Defense for Partnership Strategy and Stability Operations, *Department of Defense Support to Foreign Disaster Relief (Handbook for JTF Commanders and Below)*, Washington, D.C., GTA 90-01-030, July 13, 2011. As of May 20, 2013:
http://www.fas.org/irp/doddir/dod/disaster.pdf

Office of the Deputy Secretary of Defense, *Foreign Disaster Relief*, Washington, D.C., Department of Defense Directive 5100.46, July 6, 2012. As of May 20, 2013:
http://www.dtic.mil/whs/directives/corres/pdf/510046p.pdf

Office of the Under Secretary of Defense for Personnel and Readiness, *Military Health Support for Stability Operations*, Washington, D.C., Department of Defense Instruction 6000.16, May 17, 2010. As of May 20, 2013:
http://www.dtic.mil/whs/directives/corres/pdf/600016p.pdf

Office of the Under Secretary of Defense for Policy, *Foreign Consequence Management (FCM)*, Washington, D.C., Department of Defense Instruction 2000.21, March 10, 2006. As of May 20, 2013:
http://www.dtic.mil/whs/directives/corres/pdf/200021p.pdf

———, *Humanitarian and Civic Assistance (HCA) Activities*, Washington, D.C., Department of Defense Instruction 2205.02, December 2, 2008. As of May 20, 2013:
http://www.dtic.mil/whs/directives/corres/pdf/220502p.pdf

———, *Stability Operations*, Washington, D.C., Department of Defense Instruction 3000.05, September 16, 2009. As of May 20, 2013:
http://www.dtic.mil/whs/directives/corres/pdf/300005p.pdf

Operation Unified Response, "Humanitarian Assistance Coordination Center: Command Brief," briefing, undated.

Pendleton, John, *Defense Management: U.S. Southern Command Demonstrates Interagency Collaboration, but Its Haiti Disaster Response Revealed Challenges Conducting a Large Military Operation*, Washington, D.C.: U.S. Government Accountability Office, GAO-10-801, July 2010. As of May 17, 2013:
http://purl.fdlp.gov/GPO/gpo9589

Perry, Charles M., and Marina Travayiakis, *The U.S. Foreign Disaster Response Process: How It Works and How It Could Work Better*, Cambridge, Mass.: Institute for Foreign Policy Analysis, May 2008. As of May 20, 2013:
http://www.ifpa.org/pdf/DisasterRelief.pdf

Project on National Security Reform, *Forging a New Shield*, Arlington, Va.: Center for the Study of the Presidency, November 2008. As of May 17, 2013:
http://purl.access.gpo.gov/GPO/LPS106470

Public Law 87-195, Foreign Assistance Act, November 3, 1961.

Pueschel, Matt, "Response to Haiti May Become Model for Disaster Relief," *Military Health System*, April 26, 2010. As of May 17, 2013:
http://www.health.mil/News_And_Multimedia/News/detail/10-04-26/Response_to_Haiti_May_Become_Model_for_Disaster_Relief.aspx

Schear, James, Deputy Assistant Secretary of Defense for Partnership Strategic and Stability Operations, "National Security, Interagency Collaboration, and Lessons from SOUTHCOM and AFRICOM," testimony before the Subcommittee on National Security and Foreign Affairs, Committee on Oversight and Government Reform, U.S. House of Representatives, Washington, D.C., July 28, 2010. As of May 17, 2013:
http://www.gpo.gov/fdsys/pkg/CHRG-111hhrg64927/html/CHRG-111hhrg64927.htm

Serafino, Nina M., *The Department of Defense Role in Foreign Assistance: Background, Major Issues, and Options for Congress*, Washington, D.C.: Congressional Research Service, RL34639, December 9, 2008. As of May 17, 2013:
http://www.fas.org/sgp/crs/natsec/RL34639.pdf

SOUTHCOM—*See* U.S. Southern Command.

Telligent, "Department of Defense's APAN Leverages Community Technology to Aid in Disaster Relief," 2010. As of July 13, 2011:
http://telligent.com/files/media/CSS/Telligent_APAN_case_study_FINAL.pdf

United Nations Stabilization Mission in Haiti, "Haiti Earthquake: One Year Anniversary," undated (a). As of July 23, 2011:
http://www.un.org/en/peacekeeping/missions/minustah/rememberance.shtml

———, "Joint Operations and Tasking Centre," briefing, undated (b).

———, "MINUSTAH Background," undated (c). As of July 23, 2011:
http://www.un.org/en/peacekeeping/missions/minustah/background.shtml

———, "MINUSTAH Mandate," undated (d). As of July 23, 2011:
http://www.un.org/en/peacekeeping/missions/minustah/mandate.shtml

———, "Haiti Joint Operations and Tasking Center: Outline for Requests for Military or Police Assistance," briefing, February 1, 2010.

"U.S. Agency for International Development (USAID)," *USA.gov*, last updated June 13, 2013. Referenced May 28, 2013. As of June 14, 2013:
http://www.usa.gov/directory/federal/agency-for-inter-development.shtml

U.S. Agency for International Development, "About USAID," date unknown. Referenced July 15, 2011.

———, Bureau for Democracy, Conflict, and Humanitarian Assistance, Office of U.S. Foreign Disaster Assistance, *Field Operations Guide for Disaster Assessment and Response*, version 4.0, Washington, D.C., September 2005. As of May 20, 2013: http://transition.usaid.gov/our_work/humanitarian_assistance/disaster_assistance/resources/pdf/fog_v4.pdf

———, "New USAID Mission Director for Haiti Sworn In," Washington, D.C., press release, January 6, 2010a. As of May 17, 2013: http://www.usaid.gov/news-information/press-releases/new-usaid-mission-director-haiti-sworn

———, "Haiti: Earthquake," Washington, D.C., Fact Sheet 1, January 13, 2010b.

———, "HHS Activates Additional Components of National Disaster Medical System to Help U.S. Hospitals Treat Survivors of Earthquake in Haiti," Washington, D.C., press release, February 1, 2010c. As of May 17, 2013: http://www.usaid.gov/news-information/press-releases/hhs-activates-additional-components-national-disaster-medical-system

———, "Haiti: Earthquake," Washington, D.C., Fact Sheet 57, June 4, 2010d.

———, "Organization," last updated January 11, 2013a. As of May 20, 2013: http://www.usaid.gov/who-we-are/organization

———, home page, last updated May 10, 2013b. Referenced May 29, 2013. As of June 14, 2013: http://www.usaid.gov/home?qt-front_page_quick_tab=1

USAID—*See* U.S. Agency for International Development.

U.S. Air Force, "Joint Task Force Caring Response Brings Help to Burmese Citizens," May 21, 2008. As of May 20, 2013: http://www.af.mil/news/story.asp?id=123099682

U.S. Code, Title 10, Armed Forces, Subtitle A, General Military Law, Part I, Organization and General Military Powers, Chapter 20, Humanitarian and Other Assistance, Section 401, Humanitarian and Civic Assistance Provided in Conjunction with Military Operations.

———, Title 10, Armed Forces, Subtitle A, General Military Law, Part I, Organization and General Military Powers, Chapter 20, Humanitarian and Other Assistance, Section 402, Transportation of Humanitarian Relief Supplies to Foreign Countries.

———, Title 10, Armed Forces, Subtitle A, General Military Law, Part I, Organization and General Military Powers, Chapter 20, Humanitarian and Other Assistance, Section 404, Foreign Disaster Assistance.

———, Title 10, Armed Forces, Subtitle A, General Military Law, Part IV, Service, Supply, and Procurement, Chapter 152, Issue of Supplies, Services, and Facilities, Section 2557, Excess Nonlethal Supplies: Availability for Humanitarian Relief, Domestic Emergency Assistance, and Homeless Veterans Assistance.

———, Title 10, Armed Forces, Subtitle A, General Military Law, Part IV, Service, Supply, and Procurement, Chapter 152, Issue of Supplies, Services, and Facilities, Section 2561, Humanitarian Assistance.

———, Title 22, Foreign Relations and Intercourse, Chapter 32, Foreign Assistance, Subchapter I, International Development, Part I, Declaration of Policy, Development Assistance Authorizations, Section 2151, Congressional Findings and Declaration of Policy.

———, Title 22, Foreign Relations and Intercourse, Chapter 32, Foreign Assistance, Subchapter I, International Development, Part IX, International Disaster Assistance, Section 2292, General Provisions.

———, Title 22, Foreign Relations and Intercourse, Chapter 38, Department of State, Section 2656, Management of Foreign Affairs.

———, Title 22, Foreign Relations and Intercourse, Chapter 74, Foreign Affairs Agencies Consolidation, Subchapter V, Agency for International Development, Part B, Authorities of Secretary of State, Section 6592, Administrator of AID Reporting to Secretary of State.

———, Title 31, Money and Finance, Subtitle II, The Budget Process, Chapter 15, Appropriation Accounting, Subchapter III, Transfers and Reimbursements, Section 1535, Agency Agreements.

U.S. Customs and Border Protection, "CBP's Humanitarian Aid Exemplifies Interagency, International Coordination," January 25, 2010. As of May 17, 2013: http://www.cbp.gov/xp/cgov/newsroom/highlights/2010/haiti_relief/interagency.xml

U.S. Department of Defense, *Functions of the Department of Defense and Its Major Components*, Washington, D.C., Department of Defense Directive 5100.01, December 21, 2010. As of May 17, 2013:
http://www.dtic.mil/whs/directives/corres/pdf/510001p.pdf

U.S. Department of State, "Office of U.S. Foreign Assistance Resources," undated. Referenced August 25, 2011. As of May 17, 2013:
http://www.state.gov/f/index.htm

———, *Haiti: One Year Later: Report by the Office of the Haiti Special Coordinator*, Washington, D.C., January 10, 2011a.

———, *Congressional Budget Justification*, Vol. 2: *Foreign Operations Fiscal Year 2012*, Washington, D.C., March 2011b. As of August 25, 2011:
http://www.state.gov/documents/organization/158267.pdf

U.S. Department of State and U.S. Agency for International Development, *Strategic Plan Fiscal Years 2007–2012*, Washington, D.C., May 7, 2007. As of June 17, 2013:
http://www.state.gov/s/d/rm/rls/dosstrat/2007/index.htm

U.S. Department of State and USAID—*See* U.S. Department of State and U.S. Agency for International Development.

U.S. Geological Survey, "Earthquakes with 50,000 or More Deaths," January 2012 version. Referenced January 6, 2013. As of May 20, 2013:
http://earthquake.usgs.gov/earthquakes/world/most_destructive.php

USJFCOM—*See* U.S. Joint Forces Command.

U.S. Joint Forces Command, "Operation Unified Response Haiti Earthquake Response," Norfolk, Va.: Joint Center for Operational Analysis, May 15, 2010.

U.S. Pacific Command, "Standing Joint Force Headquarters: Pacific," undated.

———, "Joint Interagency Task Force West," current as of March 2013. Referenced May 20, 2013. As of June 14, 2013:
http://www.pacom.mil/organization/staff-directorates/jiatf-west/

U.S. Southern Command, "Narrative History of Operation Unified Response," May 25, 2010.

"The World's Worst Natural Disasters: Calamities of the 20th and 21st Centuries," CBC News, August 30, 2010. As of May 20, 2013:
http://www.cbc.ca/news/world/story/2008/05/08/f-natural-disasters-history.html

White House, "National Security Council," undated. Referenced August 26, 2011. As of May 17, 2013:
http://www.whitehouse.gov/administration/eop/nsc/

———, "United States Government Haiti Earthquake Disaster Response," Washington, D.C., press release, March 10, 2010. As of July 22, 2011:
http://www.whitehouse.gov/the-press-office/
united-states-government-haiti-earthquake-disaster-response